Windows 10 Plain & Simple

Nancy Muir Boysen

PUBLISHED BY
Microsoft Press
A division of Microsoft Corporation
One Microsoft Way
Redmond, Washington 98052-6399

Library of Congress Control Number: 2014951857
ISBN: 978-0-7356-9794-2

Printed and bound in the United States of America.

First Printing

Microsoft Press books are available through booksellers and distributors worldwide. If you need support related to this book, email Microsoft Press Support at mspinput@microsoft.com. Please tell us what you think of this book at http://aka.ms/tellpress.

This book is provided "as-is" and expresses the author's views and opinions. The views, opinions and information expressed in this book, including URL and other Internet website references, may change without notice.

Some examples depicted herein are provided for illustration only and are fictitious. No real association or connection is intended or should be inferred.

Acquisitions Editor: Rosemary Caperton
Developmental Editor: Carol Dillingham
Project Editor: Carol Dillingham
Editorial Production: Dianne Russell, Octal Publishing, Inc.
Technical Reviewer: Randall Galloway; Technical Review services provided by Content Master, a member of CM Group, Ltd.
Copyeditor: Bob Russell, Octal Publishing, Inc.
Indexer: Ellen Troutman, Octal Publishing, Inc.
Cover: Twist Creative • Seattle

Contents

Enjoying music **157**

Recording and watching videos **167**

24 Troubleshooting 269

Acknowledgments

I'd like to thank Rosemary Caperton at Microsoft Press for trusting me with the writing of this book. Also, much gratitude to Carol Dillingham, who managed the editorial aspects of the book with great grace and professionalism. Many thanks to the folks at Octal Publishing who handled with great competence all the day-to-day production work on this challenging visual book. Thanks to Ed Bott for providing assistance with select figures. Finally, thanks to my technical reviewer, Randall Galloway, for keeping me on track with Windows 10.

About this book

With Windows 10, Microsoft has created a brand new computing experience, the culmination of all of the Windows products throughout the years. Before Windows 10, you might have used any number of earlier versions, such as Windows 8.1, Windows 8, Windows 7, or Windows Vista. This book is designed to help you make the leap and understand how to find what you need and get things done. Knowing the ins and outs of working with Windows 10 will help you to be more efficient when working with your computer.

In this book, you'll find a visual learning experience that offers step-by-step instructions along with images of Windows screens and callouts for each step. You'll always know where to take an action because you can see just what to click or select in apps, the Windows 10 desktop, Start menu, and so on.

If you're new to Windows, PCs, and Windows Phones, this book will get you going. If you have used previous versions of Windows, you're going to appreciate this very powerful operating system that offers a wealth of functionality and, in many cases, fun and connections with others.

In this section:

- A quick overview
- A few assumptions
- What's new in Windows 10?
- The final word

A quick overview

Windows 10 Plain & Simple is organized into sections. Each section concerns a specific facet of Windows, and each has a color-coded bar across the top of the page; those colors match the section name in the table of contents. To help you find your way around the contents, here's a quick overview of what each section covers.

Section 2, "First look at Windows 10," is all about introducing you to the various visual interfaces of Windows 10, such as the Desktop, Start menu, Task View, and Action Center. You also learn how to start Windows 10, log in to your account, and shut down Windows.

Section 3, "Navigating Windows 10," helps you to create other user accounts if your computer is used by people other than you, how to add passwords, and how to open the Windows Settings app, where you can control a variety of features. You are also introduced to Cortana, the personal assistant and search feature new to Windows 10. You get a closer look at the

elements on the Start menu, which you use to access apps and settings. Along the way, you get advice about using the taskbar, Task View, setting the date and time, and managing power and storage options.

Section 4, "Customizing the appearance of Windows 10," is the section where you discover the ways in which you can make Windows look the way you prefer. In this section, you adjust desktop themes, colors, background, and text. You change your screen saver, change screen resolution, and customize the task-bar. In addition, you work with tiles in the Start menu.

Section 5, "Working with productivity applications," explores working with applications such as Microsoft Word, Excel, and Power-Point. You discover how to open, close, and uninstall apps, as well as how to work with app features such as menus and toolbars. In this section, you also learn about saving, sharing, and printing files.

Section 6, "Finding content with File Explorer and Cortana," is all about finding what you need, both on your computer and online. You find your way around File Explorer, the Windows app that helps you to move through the hierarchy of files and folders on your computer and storage drives. You use Cortana to search your computer for files, apps, or settings, and search the web for just about anything.

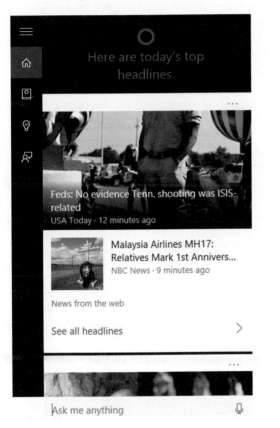

Section 7, "Making Windows accessible," is all about features that make it easier to work on a computer if you have vision, hearing, or dexterity challenges. Here, you learn about adjusting screen contrast and brightness, modifying mouse and keyboard settings to make them easier to handle, using Speech Recognition, Narrator, and more.

Section 8, "Accessing and managing networks," contains tasks that get you up to speed on networking basics. You explore setting up your own network and connecting to a public network. You discover how to make settings to keep your network secure, and learn how to turn Airplane Mode on and off so that your laptop won't try to connect to a network while you're on a plane.

Section 9, "Going online with Microsoft Edge," introduces you to Microsoft's new browser. You learn to navigate among websites, use Reading View, and tabs. Browsing raises security concerns, so you also learn about blocking pop-up windows, clearing your browsing history, and configuring other security settings. Finally, you learn how to use Web Note, a new feature to mark-up webpages and share them.

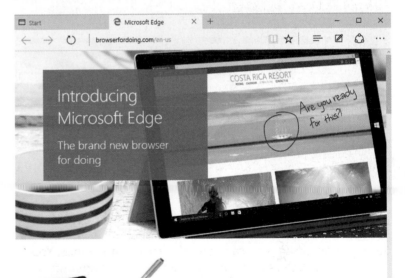

Section 10, "Connecting with others," focuses on the useful People app. This provides a contact database that lets you add and retrieve information about people and organizations with which you interact.

Section 11, "Using Mail," explores the Mail app built in to Windows 10. After you set up your email accounts in Mail, you can read messages from multiple email accounts; create, format, and send new messages; and organize email messages into folders.

Section 12, "Shopping for apps in the Windows Store," shows you how to use the Windows Store to read reviews from other users and try out apps before you buy. After you have found an app that you want to buy, this section shows you how to buy and rate that app.

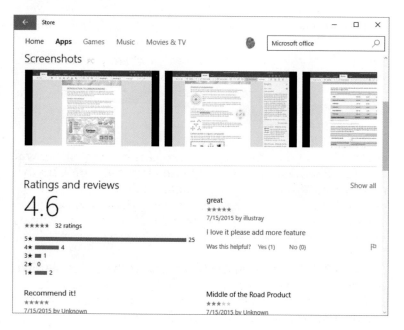

Section 13, "Enjoying music," introduces you to the Windows 10 app for buying, playing, and creating playlists of music. You also discover Cortana's ability to identify music that's playing at the moment. Finally, this section covers adjusting the volume of your device for the best listening experience.

Section 14, "Recording and watching videos," involves working with the video setting of the Camera app in conjunction with your computer's built-in camera. You explore finding movies by using the Movies & TV app, and playing those movies by using the app's playback controls. Finally, this section provides an overview of the features of Windows Media Player.

Section 15, "Working with the Camera and Photos apps," shows you how to take photos and then organize and edit them. You also explore sharing photos with others, creating a slideshow from photos, and using a photo as your Lock screen background.

Section 16, "Keeping on schedule with Calendar," helps you to explore various Calendar views, create and edit an event, and display the Holidays and Birthdays calendars. You also learn how to create a new event by using Cortana, the Windows 10 personal assistant.

Section 17, "Tracking your sports, news, stocks, and fitness," looks at several popular apps that are built in to Windows 10. You find out about adding favorite sports teams or news sources, using financial tools to track your investments and view stock market activity, and read articles about your interests.

Section 18, "Checking the weather," examines all of the features of the Windows 10 Weather app, including turning on Location and Location History, and searching for directions. You discover how to change map styles, zoom in and out, and place a pin on a map.

Section 19, "Using Maps," explores the Maps app, which helps you to get where you want to go in the world by providing directions for driving, walking, and even taking public transit. If you grant Maps permission to pinpoint your location, it can more accurately provide directions to and from your location. You can even view 3D maps of certain cities around the world.

Section 20, "Playing with Xbox games," is where you can explore the world of gaming in Windows 10. Using the Xbox app, you can buy games, add friends, and create your own gaming name and avatar. After you begin playing, you can track your achievements and send messages to your friends.

Section 21, "Adding and working with other devices," shows you how to add devices such as printers and scanners. You learn the ins and outs of connecting with Bluetooth devices (which can operate only at short range) and removing devices. Finally, you are introduced to Device Manager and find out how to change device properties and download the latest device drivers.

Section 22, "Working with OneDrive," covers the basics of using the Microsoft OneDrive online file-sharing app. You learn to create folders, upload files, search for files, share files or folders, and rename or delete content from OneDrive.

Section 23, "Maintaining and protecting your computer," looks at several procedures that are important for ensuring that you keep your data and computer protected and its systems maintained. You learn how to get manual updates for Windows 10 between automatic updates, and use tools to clear out unused files or organize data on your hard disk for better performance. You also learn about security features, including Windows Defender and Windows Firewall.

Section 24, "Troubleshooting," addresses situations in which your computer is experiencing problems. In that case, you can use tools to reset and restore your computer or get remote assistance. You can look for help, or modify startup options to reboot your computer from a USB stick or DVD drive. In the worst case, you might choose to reinstall Windows and start again.

A few assumptions

To provide the information you need but not bore you with information you already have, I've made a few assumptions. For example, I assume that you have worked with a computer before and that you know how to use a mouse and keyboard. I don't assume that you have or have used a touchscreen computer, so although I provide guidance in Section 3 on touchscreen gestures that you can use in Windows 10, most steps are described based on a mouse and keyboard combination.

I also assume that you have worked with some kind of software before, using drop-down menus, toolbars, and dialog boxes to get things done. To use this book and to get the most out of Windows 10, you should have an Internet connection and have explored the Internet in the past.

I expect that you are a visual learner who wants information provided in a straightforward, easy-to-understand style as well as tips to make you a better Windows user. No matter how technical you are, I assume that you want to get up to speed on Windows 10 quickly, and without serious effort.

What's new in Windows 10?

If you're coming from Windows 8.1 or Windows 8, some of Windows 10 will be familiar to you, such as tiles for accessing apps and improved support of touchscreens. If you're migrating from an earlier version of Windows, you'll be glad to see the familiar Start menu, albeit sporting a more graphical look.

What's new to users of all previous versions of Windows is the way that Control Panel settings—and most other settings—now reside in the Settings app. In addition, Task View displays all open apps, helping you to multitask easily. Within Task View you can create multiple desktops so that you can return to any one of them and have just the apps you want at the moment, already open on that desktop.

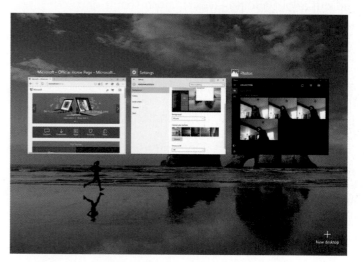

The Action Center contains notifications as well as some short-cuts to common settings such as connecting to a network, brightening the screen, or turning Location services or Airplane Mode on or off.

Perhaps the biggest news in Windows 10 is Cortana, a personal assistant and search feature that learns about your activities and preferences and provides information, search results, and even jokes on request. You can interact with Cortana verbally, or by typing a word or phrase in her Search box. You can also ask Cortana to open apps, play music, send an email, make an appointment, and much, much more.

The final word

Computers and the Internet open up a world of opportunity and entertainment. With Windows 10 and its many apps, you have an operating system that integrates functionality, creativity, and sharing in a brand new way. Whether you use your computer to listen to music, go online, write reports, or keep up with sports, Windows 10 will make your experience better. In this book I've tried to provide a user-friendly visual learning tool that will help you master Windows 10 quickly and easily.

I hope that you profit from this book and find that its design and organization enhance your learning and enjoyment.

First look at Windows 10

Windows 10 represents a leap for Microsoft, but not just from version number 8.1 to 10 (skipping 9 entirely). In fact, Windows 10 is a combination of users' favorite features for the operating system that creates the most seamless way for you to interact with your computer that Microsoft has ever provided.

With Windows 10, you find the traditional Windows desktop and Start menu integrated with features such as Task View (which you use to take a look at and switch among all open apps), the Action Center for accessing various settings and notifications, and multiple desktops so that you can construct different "ecosystems" of programs and apps for each use. Windows 10 places an emphasis on using integrated touchscreen devices such as smartphones, tablets, and touchscreen-enabled computers to make computing a very natural experience, but you can still perform any activity without a touchscreen computer by using a mouse and keyboard.

Starting Windows 10 for the first time

The first time you press the power button to turn on a computer with Windows 10 installed, you are offered some options about how to set it up. The simplest way to deal with this is to follow the directions on the screen and choose Express Settings, which include the most common configurations for working with your computer.

After you press the power button, the first screen you'll see when Windows 10 starts for the first time greets you with a cheery "Hi there." When you click Next to proceed, you'll have the option to either choose Express Settings or to customize your settings. Click Express Settings, and after a few moments, your Windows desktop appears.

> ✓ **TIP**   You can modify any of the Express Settings that Windows 10 implements, such as date, time, or language, after you begin using Windows. To modify the date, time, or language settings, click the Start button, click Settings, and then click Time & Language.

Signing in to your user account

Your user account is set up when you first start Windows 10. You can create additional user accounts for Windows so that different people who use your computer can save their unique files and Windows settings. Whether you turn off your computer or it goes to sleep after a period of inactivity, you are signed out of the currently active user account and presented with a Lock Screen. You need to type a password to sign in to Windows as the last active user or as another user. If you set up a PIN (a 4-digit code alternative to a password) in Settings, you can provide that instead of a password.

Sign in

1 Click anywhere on the Lock Screen.

2 Type the password or PIN.

Signing in with a different user account

When you have created more than one user (see Section 3, "Navigating Windows 10," for more about this), you can sign in as another user to open Windows with that person's unique settings and files. You do this from the same Windows sign-in screen that was shown in the previous task.

Sign in as a different user

1 Click the Lock Screen to display the sign-in screen.

2 Click the user name of the account to which you want to sign in.

3 Type a password to sign in as that user.

TIP To create other user accounts, on the desktop click the Start button, click Settings, and then click Accounts. You can create as many accounts as you like, each one preserving settings and documents unique to that account. You can also set up a password or PIN for signing in. See "Setting up accounts" on page 26 for details about this process.

Understanding the desktop

Whereas Windows 7 had a single desktop and Start menu, and Windows 8 had a desktop and a Start screen but no Start menu, Windows 10 strikes a happy medium; this version of Windows has a single desktop with a Start menu that you can expand to a full screen. If you'd rather stick to working primarily on the desktop, you can access common commands and apps through the redesigned Start menu.

The desktop in Windows 10 also retains the traditional task-bar along the bottom, desktop shortcuts for items such as the Recycle Bin, and a few added features, such as Cortana, the new personal assistant that can help you accomplish many tasks. When turned on (which it is by default), Cortana appears on the left side of the taskbar and looks like a search box in which you can enter a search term and get results related to files on your computer or content on the web. But Cortana offers much more. You can wake Cortana by saying, "Hey, Cortana," or by clicking the microphone button on the right side of the Cortana search box. You can also type a question or term in the box and Cortana will find matching results. If you turn off the Cortana feature, the box acts as a straightforward search tool.

To the right of the Cortana search box is the Task View button that you can click to view all open apps on the desk-top, side by side, helping you to switch among them quickly. Finally, the new Action Center button, located on the right side of the taskbar, opens the Action Center, which is a slide-out panel that lists notifications about items such as new email or upcoming appointments. It also offers an expand-able set of buttons that provide access to Windows settings.

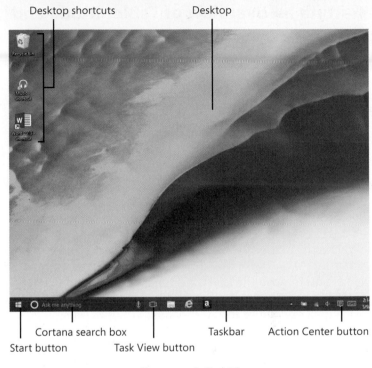

Desktop shortcuts · Desktop

Cortana search box · Taskbar · Action Center button
Start button · Task View button

Open apps in Task View

Getting an overview of Tablet Mode and Continuum

One of the settings you access through the Action Center is Tablet Mode. Tablet Mode makes it possible to work with a touchscreen interface without having to use a physical keyboard or mouse. Tablet Mode displays open apps in a full-screen view rather than in windows. In addition, when Tablet Mode is active and you click the Start button, the expanded Start menu is displayed.

You can display Tablet Mode on any computer, not just a tablet. When you work with a Windows tablet such as Microsoft Surface or if you have a laptop that converts to a tablet configuration (a 2-in-1 model in which the screen detaches from the keyboard), this mode is very handy.

When you remove the keyboard functionality from a tablet or laptop, the Continuum feature kicks in automatically, displaying all open apps in Tablet Mode.

Full-screen version of the Start menu

App tile

Full-screen version of an app in Tablet Mode

Tablet Mode button

Using the Start menu

The Start menu provides access to such popular items as File Explorer, Documents, and Settings, as well as your most frequently used apps. In addition, the Start menu offers a Power button that you can use to put your computer to sleep, restart it, or turn it off altogether. The Start menu also contains tiles that will be familiar to users of the Windows 8 and Windows 8.1

Start Screen; you can click these to access apps such as News, Camera, Music, Mail, and Calendar. You can also use the Start menu to display a list of All Apps or expand the menu to a full-screen view. (Note that if you are in Tablet Mode—described in the previous task—the Start menu opens to a full-screen view by default; the following steps assume that Tablet Mode is off).

Display the Start menu

1   Click the Start button.

2   In the list on the left, click a recently used app.

3   Click the Start button again.

4   Click an app tile.

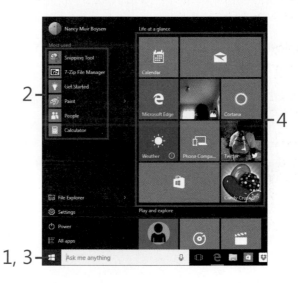

> **TIP**   You can add labels (which you can later edit) to the sets of tiles to help you identify their content. Click above a set of tiles and then, in the text box that appears, type a label, such as Online Content or Lifestyle Apps. Click anywhere outside of the text box to accept the new label.

Viewing All Apps

The Start menu shows you the most recently used apps (on the left side of the screen) and several commonly used apps in tiles. However, not all apps are included in these lists. To find any app, you can display an alphabetical list of all installed apps, scroll to find the one you need, and then click to open it.

Display All Apps

1 Click the Start button.

2 Click All Apps.

3 Click an app to open it.

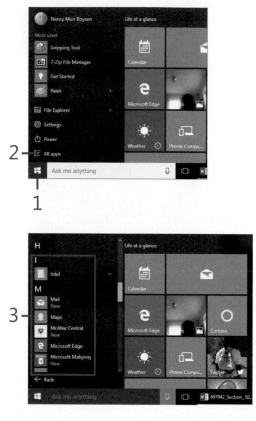

Working with Task View

With Task View, you can view thumbnails of all open apps and switch among them with ease. If, for example, you are using Microsoft Word and you want to make a call on Skype, which you had opened earlier, you can go to Task View without closing

Word and jump to the Skype app to make your call. When your call is over, you can use Task View to quickly jump back to the still-open Word app.

Open Task View and switch among open apps

1   On the taskbar, click the Task View button.

2   Click an app to make it the active app.

 TIP   An alternative to using the Task View button is to press Alt+Tab on your keyboard. A box appears containing all open apps. While continuing to hold down the Alt key, click Tab to scroll among the open apps.

Using multiple desktops

New in Windows 10 is the ability to create and save multiple desktops. For example, you might like to have one set of apps that you use for your hobby and another for your work, but you want to keep those sets of open apps separate. You can create one desktop that displays open apps related to your hobby, another related to the apps you use for work, and so on. You then can easily switch among them.

Create and display a desktop

1 On the taskbar, click the Task View button.

2 Click New Desktop.

3 Open any apps that you want to appear on this desktop by using the Start menu (click an item in the Most Used section of the app list, All Apps, or a tile).

4 To cycle among the desktops, click the Task View button.

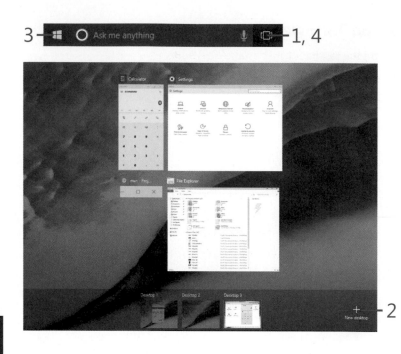

> **TRY THIS** Use the method described here to create a desktop for work-related apps, another for your family's activities, and another for a hobby such as genealogy or stamp collecting. Show your family or friends how to switch among these desktops.

> **TIP** To delete a desktop click the Task View button, and then, in the top-right corner of any desktop displayed, click the Close button.

Opening the Action Center

The Action Center is a useful panel that's new with Windows 10. When you display the Action Center, you see notifications about items such as new email or upcoming appointments as well as a set of buttons with which you can access all Windows settings, or switch on or off several commonly used settings such as Tablet Mode, Airplane Mode, and Bluetooth device connections. You can also adjust settings for Brightness.

Display the Action Center

1 On the taskbar, click the Action Center button.

2 Click a notification to see more details.

3 Click a setting.

You will see different results depending on which setting you choose:

- Click a setting button to turn it on or off (as with Tablet Mode, Bluetooth, Airplane Mode, Rotation Lock, Wi-Fi, and Location sharing).

- Click a setting button to display a panel for working with those types of settings (as with Connect, All Settings, and VPN).

- The Brightness setting increases the brightness of your screen with each click. For more control over screen brightness, right-click the Brightness button, and then, in the shortcut menu that appears, click Go To Settings to open a window with display settings, including a Brightness Level slider.

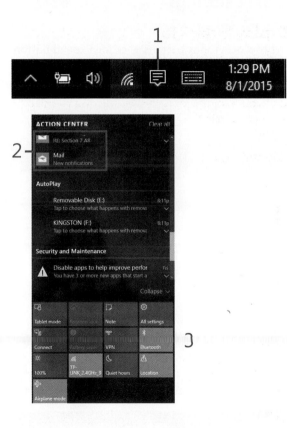

Working with settings in the Action Center

If you want to display only the most frequently used settings buttons in the Action Center, you can collapse the set of settings buttons to show less. You then can easily expand this area of the Action Center to display all settings buttons.

Expand and select settings

1 On the taskbar, click the Action Center button.

2 If there is only one row of settings buttons, click the Expand button to display all settings.

3 Click the Collapse button to show only the top row of settings.

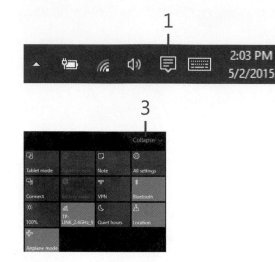

✓ **TIP** The All Settings button is your entrée to all Windows settings. See "Accessing Settings" on page 25 to learn more about what this button makes available to you.

Shutting down Windows 10

When you're done working with your computer, you have a few options. You can use the Power button, which is located in the Start menu, to turn off your computer, restart it (which is useful when installing new software or implementing software updates), or put it to sleep. Putting your computer to sleep saves power when you're not using your computer, but let's you get going quickly when you want to use your computer again.

Work with the Power button

1 Click the Start button.

2 Click Power.

3 Click the option you want: Sleep to temporarily put your computer to sleep; Shut Down to turn off your computer; or Restart to turn off and then turn on your computer (for example, to allow updates to be implemented).

> ✓ **TIP** You can use the Restart option if your computer or an app seems to be experiencing problems. Restarting causes Windows to reboot, which can often solve performance issues. See Section 24, "Troubleshooting," for more about solving computer problems.

Navigating
Windows 10

Beginning to use a new operating system such as Windows 10 is like walking into a new job: You need to figure out where your desk is, where the copier and coffee are, and how to find your coworkers. In Windows you need to learn how to open and close applications; set up user accounts and passwords so that more than one person can access your computer; provide input with a mouse, keyboard, or touchscreen; and learn how to find and use some of the basic settings and tools that are available to you.

After you explore the tasks in this section, you'll know the basics of getting around Windows 10, making settings, providing input, and searching for information by using the exciting new personal assistant, Cortana. You also encounter the taskbar, which provides shortcuts to various functions, and the Start menu, which gives you access to all of your apps.

In this section:

- Opening and closing windows
- Accessing Settings
- Setting up accounts
- Managing passwords
- Adding a picture password
- Using a PIN
- Using a touchscreen with Windows 10
- Exploring the Start menu
- Expanding the Start menu
- Exploring the taskbar
- Working with Cortana
- Adjusting system volume
- Managing power options
- Setting the date and time

Opening and closing windows

There's a good reason why the Windows operating system has its name. When you work with this operating system, you open *windows* to display applications such as Microsoft Word, media players, Internet browsers, files and folders, settings, and more. When you open a window, you can use all the tools and features of that environment. You can also display a window as full screen or in a reduced size (which helps you to work with more than one app at a time), and you can close a window, which closes the application.

Work with windows

1 Click the Start button.

2 Click the Calendar tile.

3 Click the Maximize button.

4 Click the Minimize button.

5 Click the Close button.

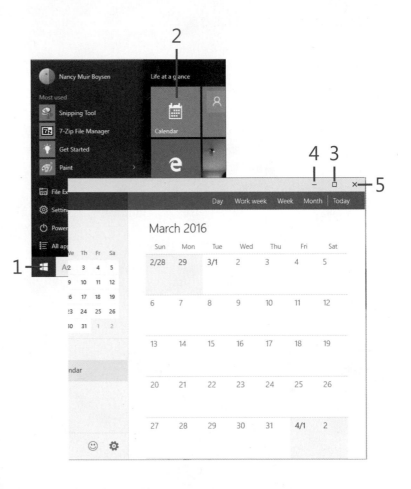

> **TIP**   You can display several reduced windows on your desktop. If you want to view all open apps, on the taskbar, click the Task View button, which then displays all open apps in thumbnails, whether the apps are open full screen or reduced to a smaller window.

> **TRY THIS**   With a window open, click the Minimize button (it's represented by the dash symbol to the left of the Maximize/ Minimize button in the top-right corner of the window). This keeps the app open and available on the taskbar, but the app window does not display on the screen.

Accessing Settings

In addition to applications, Windows 10 offers its own settings that help you to set up new user accounts, open accessibility tools such as Narrator; manage your system, network, and devices; and personalize the look of your desktop and windows.

The Settings window is also where you can manage your computer's security and set up the date, time, and language, as well as perform updates to Windows. Consider this like the central command for Windows 10.

Open and close Settings

1 Click the Start button.

2 Click Settings.

3 Click any category of Settings to display a secondary Settings window for that category.

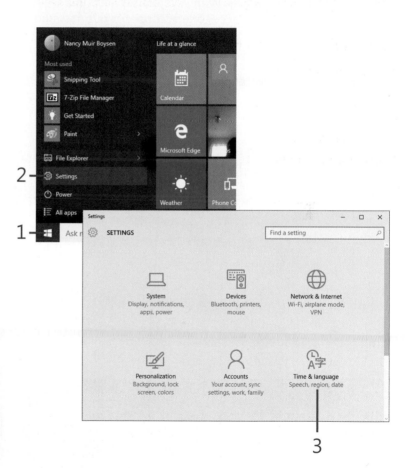

> **TIP** You can also display Settings by using a keystroke short-cut. To do so, on your keyboard, press the Windows logo key+I simultaneously.

> **TIP** If you used earlier versions of Windows you might have become familiar with the Control Panel. The settings you found there are now available in Settings and its secondary windows.

Setting up accounts

In many instances, there might be more than one person using a computer, or you might want to use it for more than one purpose. You can set up separate user accounts within which you can save unique settings (such as desktop background), sets of applications, and files. With several user accounts set up, you can, for example, access one account for business and one for personal use, or one for you and one for your spouse.

You can even password-protect accounts so that nobody can open another person's account, thereby preventing your child or brother-in-law from accessing and deleting your valuable investment spreadsheet or novel. When you first set up Windows 10, a user account is created for you. You can add accounts at any time so long as you're logged-in to an account with administrator privileges.

Add a new user account

1 Display Settings.

2 Click Accounts.

3 Click Family & Other Users.

4 Click Add Someone Else To This PC.

(continued on next page)

Add a new user account *(continued)*

5 Type an email address that the new person will use to sign in to Windows 10, if you know it.

6 Click Next.

7 Click Finish.

How will this person sign in?

Enter the email address of the person you want to add. If they use Xbox Live, Outlook.com, Windows, or OneDrive, enter the email address they use to sign in.

5 ——| Email or phone |

The person I want to add doesn't have an email address

Privacy statement

6 ——[Next] [Cancel]

7 ——[Finish]

> **TIP** If you are creating an account for a child and want to use Family Safety settings to get reports on the child's activities on the computer, select the check box labeled Is This A Child's Account? before you click Finish in step 7.

Managing passwords

Each user account that you create on your computer can have its own separate settings and files. For privacy, and to avoid somebody damaging your files or changing your settings inadvertently, you can protect each user account with a password.

With a password set, only those who know the password can open a user account. The following steps describe how to change the password; these instructions apply to the account to which you are currently signed in.

Change a password

1 Go to the Accounts section of Settings, and then click Sign-In Options.

2 In the Password section, click Change.

3 Type your password to verify your identity, and then click Sign In.

(continued on next page)

Change a password *(continued)*

4 Type your old password.

5 Type and confirm your new password, and then click Next.

6 Click Finish.

4— ┤ Old password

Forgot your password?

Change your Microsoft account password

Create password ———————————— —5

Reenter password ————————

Next   Cancel

6— Finish

✓ **TIP**   Be aware that changing your Microsoft account password on your Windows computer changes the password you use to access that account online; for example, to access your Microsoft email account.

Adding a picture password

If you're more of the visual type and have a touchscreen computer, you might prefer to access your account by using a picture rather than by using password characters. With the picture password, you select a picture and then assign three onscreen gestures. For example, if you use a picture of a person, you might draw a smile on the lips and circles around the eyes. The combination of the picture and your gestures thereby become your password.

Create a picture password

1 In Settings, click Account, and then click Sign-In Options.

2 In the Picture Password section, click Add.

3 In the Password box, type your current password.

4 Click OK.

5 Click Choose Picture.

(continued on next page)

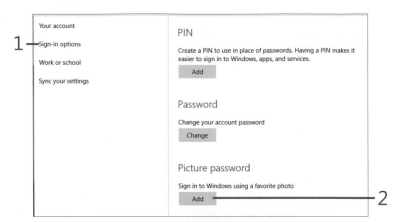

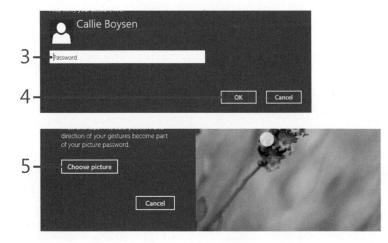

Create a picture password (continued)

6 In the File Name box, type a name or browse through your files to find a picture to use.

7 Click Open.

8 Click Use This Picture.

9 Using your finger, draw gestures on the touchscreen.

10 Repeat the gestures to confirm them.

11 Click Finish.

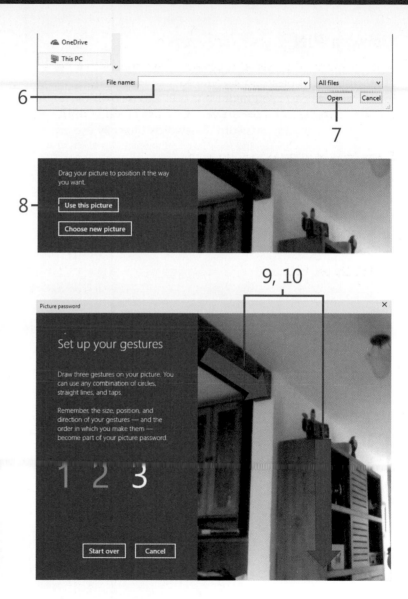

✅ **TIP** If you decide that you no longer want to use a Picture Password, in the Accounts window, click the Remove button, located in the Picture Password section.

⚠ **CAUTION** You must remember your picture password gestures, including the approximate start and end points and the direction to swipe. If you forget your gestures, you won't be able to access your account.

Using a PIN

Passwords are very useful, but sometimes they contain more characters than you'd care to type each and every time you sign in. If that's the case, you might find a PIN to be very useful. A PIN is a four-digit password, which is typically much shorter and easier to type than a password. Passwords typically use eight or more characters, combining letters, numbers, symbols, and upper and lowercase letters; however, as a result of those extra characters and the combinations that you can use, a password is a more secure means of protecting your device.

Create a PIN

1 Display Settings.

2 Click Accounts.

(continued on next page)

Create a PIN *(continued)*

3 Click Sign-In Options.

4 In the PIN section, click Add.

5 Type your four-digit PIN.

6 Confirm the PIN.

7 Click OK.

TIP If you clear the Use A Simple PIN check box, you can set a PIN that's longer than four digits.

Using a touchscreen with Windows 10

If you have a touchscreen computer, you can take advantage of several ways in which Windows 10 is optimized for touch input. Using your finger and touch gestures in place of a mouse or keyboard, you can scroll down a page, make a selection, choose a command or check box, and type using an onscreen keyboard. This natural way of interacting with a touchscreen computer is efficient—no batteries or cords required.

Here is a list of commonly used touchscreen gestures that you can utilize with your Windows 10 computer:

- Tap to select any item that you'd click with a mouse, such as a check box, drop-down list, on/off switch, or text box. You can also tap to place an insertion point in a document, indicating where the next action is to take place.

> ✓ **TIP** In Windows 10, several multifinger gestures were introduced for use on laptops that have touchpads built in. For example, swiping the touchpad with three fingers displays the Cortana panel, and swiping the touchpad with four fingers opens Action Center.

> ✓ **TIP** Because not everybody has a touchscreen-enabled computer, most of the steps in this book assume the use of a mouse and keyboard, but feel free to substitute a tap whenever a step instructs you to click!

- Swipe your finger from the left edge of the screen inward to display Task View.

- Swipe your finger from the right edge of the screen inward to display the Action Center.

- Place your fingers together on the screen and spread them apart to enlarge a document or webpage.

- Place your fingers apart on the screen and pinch them together to reduce a document or webpage.

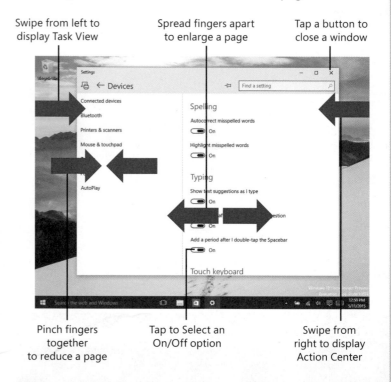

Swipe from left to display Task View

Spread fingers apart to enlarge a page

Tap a button to close a window

Pinch fingers together to reduce a page

Tap to Select an On/Off option

Swipe from right to display Action Center

Exploring the Start menu

The Start menu provides access to all of the apps and settings that are available on your Windows 10 computer. At the bottom of the Start menu, there are four frequently used items that are always available: File Explorer (for locating files and folders), Settings, Power, and All Apps. In addition you can click All Apps to display an alphabetical list of all the apps on your computer. The items you use most often appear in a list on the left of the menu. To the right are sets of tiles that you can click to explore popular apps such as Music, News, and Mail.

Open and make choices from the Start menu

1 Click the Start button.

2 Click All Apps.

3 From the list, select an app to open it.

4 Click the Start button again.

5 Click an app tile, such as Weather.

6 Click the Start button again.

7 Click Power to view a menu of options.

8 Click outside of the Power menu to close it.

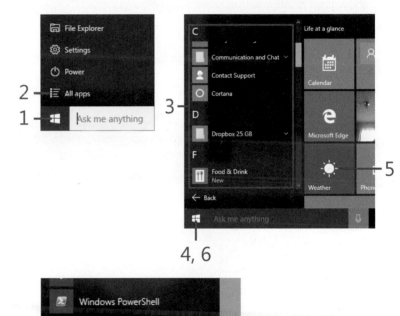

 TRY THIS Tiles in the Start menu are organized into groups; for example, Life At A Glance. If you want to rename a group, press and hold the space above a set of tiles. The Title box opens, in which you can type a new name for the tiles in that group.

Expanding the Start menu

You can display the Start menu in full screen. This way, you can see more app tiles on the screen and more easily rearrange or resize the tiles. The full-screen display remains in effect until you restore it to the smaller version.

Open the Start menu full screen

1 With Settings displayed, click Personalization.

2 Click Start.

3 Click the Use Start Full Screen switch to turn it on.

4 Click the Close button.

> **TIP** If you put your computer in Tablet Mode—which you might do if you were using a touchscreen device—only the expanded Start menu appears. To turn on Tablet Mode, open Action Center, and then tap the Tablet Mode setting.

Exploring the taskbar

By default, the taskbar runs across the bottom of the Windows desktop (you can change its location on the screen, which I'll show you how to do in Section 4, "Customizing the appearance of Windows 10"). This small bar contains a wealth of settings, making them available for quick and easy access. It also shows active applications whose windows have been minimized so that you can simply click one to enlarge it. If the taskbar isn't visible, move your mouse pointer to the bottom of the desktop to display it.

The Start button is on the far left of the taskbar. You click this to display the Start menu, from which you can access all the apps installed on your computer. Directly to the right of the Start button is Cortana, the new personal assistant and search feature (covered in the next task).

You use the buttons in the middle of the taskbar to display open apps in Task View or maximize open apps.

Finally, the set of buttons on the right side of the taskbar give you access to settings for features such as power management, network connections, system volume, Action Center, and the Touch Keyboard. You can use the Show Hidden Icons button to display more available settings. Several of these items are covered in more detail later in this section. Action Center is covered in Section 2, "First look at Windows 10," and network settings are covered in Section 8, "Accessing and managing networks."

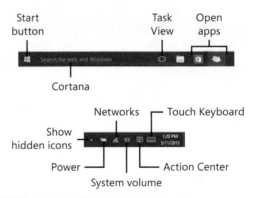

TIP If you want the taskbar to remain on the screen at all times, right-click the Show Hidden Icons button, and then, from the shortcut menu that appears, select Lock The Taskbar.

Working with Cortana

Cortana is a new personal assistant feature in Windows 10 that serves many functions. Using Cortana, you can search for all kinds of items, including files on your computer, online information, and media. Cortana also gives you an overview of your day, which might include appointments, news headlines, local events, and even a suggested restaurant for lunch. In fact, Cortana learns about you as you interact with your computer, so her suggestions become more and more relevant. You can ask Cortana to send an email message or place a call via Skype. Cortana provides two means of input: You can type a word, phrase, or question into the Cortana search box, or you can speak to Cortana and, depending on what you type or say, she will either respond verbally or by displaying search results. Note that the first time you open Cortana, you are asked for permission to let her access your computer and record your name so that she can greet you by name.

When you ask Cortana for anything, a panel appears with results as well as a set of buttons that you can use to do the following:

- View a Notebook home page that you can customize to contain items you use often, such as travel information, news headlines, and weather.

- Access saved reminders and create new reminders.

TIP   You can ask Cortana to identify a piece of music that's playing. Just say, "Hey Cortana, what song is playing," and she'll identify it and provide a link to the Store to buy it, if you like.

Provide voice and text input for Cortana

1 Click the Cortana search box.

2 Type a word, phrase, or question.

3 At the bottom of the Cortana pane, click either the My Stuff or Web option to narrow your search.

4 Click the result that you want Cortana to display.

5 On the right side of Cortana's search box, click the microphone.

6 When the Cortana pane appears, speak a word, phrase, or question.

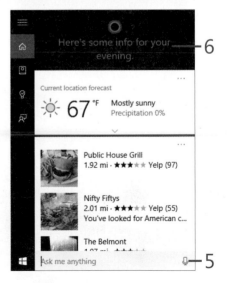

TRY THIS   Instead of clicking the microphone in the Cortana search box, try saying, "Hey Cortana," followed by a question such as, "When is my next appointment?" As you use Cortana over time, she becomes more accustomed to your voice and the items you access frequently.

TIP   You can use Cortana in many settings; for example, you can search for nearby locations such as banks by using the Notebook feature, ask her to schedule an event in Calendar, and have her identify music. Look for coverage of Cortana in other parts of the book, including "Using Cortana to identify music" on page 165, "Using Cortana to add an event" on page 195, and "Viewing favorites" on page 227.

Adjusting system volume

You've probably watched a movie or listened to music on a Windows computer before, so you know that media players have their own volume controls provided within their playback tools. However, your computer also has a system volume control. This control sets the volume of your computer, and thus the volume for individual players is set relative to that master volume (for example, a player volume set at 50 percent is set at 50 percent of the system volume setting). A handy button on the taskbar offers you control over system volume.

Raise or lower volume

1 On the right side of the taskbar, click the Volume button.

2 Drag the slider to the right to raise the volume.

3 Drag the slider to the left to lower the volume.

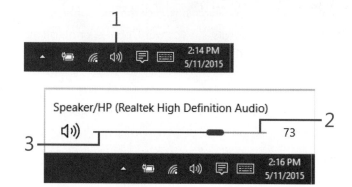

✓ **TIP** To access separate controls for your speakers and your system sounds (such as alerts for new notifications), right-click the Volume button, and then, in the shortcut menu that opens, select Open Volume Mixer.

Setting the date and time

Your computer depends on knowing the date and time in your location to do many things. For example, if you have scheduled maintenance tasks such as downloading system updates for a certain time of the day, that time is dependent on your date and time settings. Your calendar is attuned to the date and time settings, including notifications and alerts. If you travel with your computer or move to a new location, you might want to change the date and time to match your whereabouts.

Change the date and time

1   On the taskbar, right-click the Date And Time button.

2   Click Adjust Date/Time.

3   With the Set Time Automatically setting switched to Off, click the Change button under Change Date And Time.

4   Click the drop-down lists to change settings for the Date.

5   In the Time options, click the up or down arrows to change settings.

6   Click Change to close the Date And Time Settings dialog box.

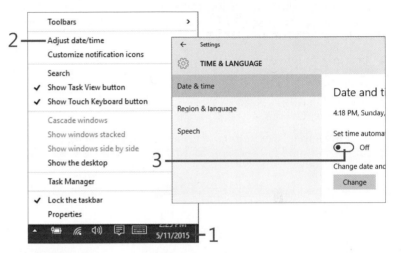

TRY THIS   If you simply want to change your time zone so that the computer adjusts date and time automatically, in step 3, you would instead click Set Time Automatically.

Managing power options

If you work on a laptop computer or tablet, you need to be aware of the remaining charge in your battery. With Windows 10, you can adjust power options so that your computer conserves energy by adjusting its performance. For example, using a Power Saver plan might maintain your screen brightness at a dimmer setting to help your battery's charge last longer. You can choose which power plan to use, ranging from

Power Saver to High Performance. Power Saver reduces your computer's performance but saves energy. High Performance lets your computer deliver the best performance, but your battery will discharge sooner. You can also adjust the timing of certain actions, such as when Windows puts the computer to sleep, by changing settings for a particular plan.

Adjust power options

1 On the taskbar, right-click the Power & Sleep Settings button.

2 Click Power Options.

3 Click the Power Saver setting to turn it on if it's not already.

4 Click Change Plan Settings.

(continued on next page)

Adjust power options *(continued)*

5 Click the On Battery drop-down list and choose the timing for turning off the display, putting the computer to sleep, and adjusting plan brightness for when the computer is running on battery.

6 Click the Plugged In drop-down list and choose the timing for turning off the display, putting the computer to sleep, and adjusting plan brightness for when the computer is plugged in.

7 Click Save Changes.

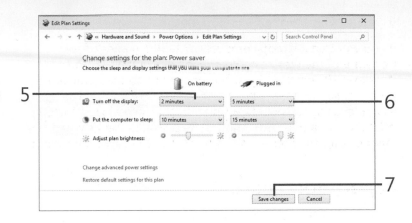

Customizing the appearance of Windows 10

Windows 10 is an environment in which you'll spend a lot of time, so being able to set up the appearance of its various elements in ways that please you is a great benefit. You can change the background image for the desktop, colors, the size of text, and more. You can also work with the size and placement of tiles in the Start menu.

Some of these settings customize the desktop appearance, whereas others make working with apps a lot easier. For example, you can arrange open windows on the desktop so that you can view more than one app at a time, which helps when you need to copy and paste contents from one app to another or reference information in one document while working in another. You can customize the taskbar contents such that the icons you need most often are always close at hand.

In this section:

- Changing the desktop background
- Customize the Lock Screen
- Using themes
- Adjusting colors and transparency
- Changing the screen saver
- Making timeout settings
- Enlarging text
- Changing screen resolution
- Customizing the taskbar
- Adding tiles to the Start menu
- Moving tiles
- Resizing tiles
- Using Snap to arrange apps on the Desktop

Changing the desktop background

We all like to personalize our work environment, from pinning photos to the wall of a cubicle at work to decorating the walls of our home office. In the same way, Windows 10 provides images that you can use to add visual appeal to your Desktop.

To customize your Windows experience, you can change which Windows images appear as backgrounds, and even use your own images.

Choose a new background picture

1 Click the Start button.

2 Click Settings.

3 Click Personalization.

4 Click Background.

5 In the Choose Your Picture section, click an option.

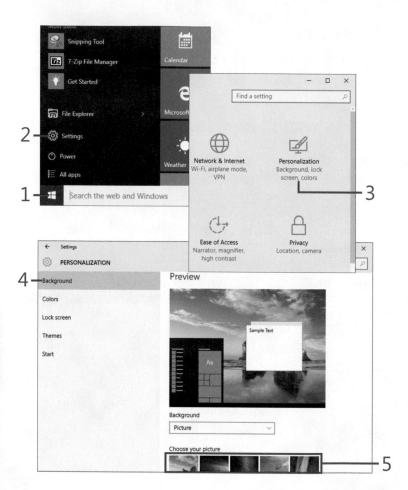

> ✓ **TIP** To select your own picture as your background in step 5, you can click the Browse button (not shown in the illustration) and then locate a picture of your own by using File Explorer. When you've found the picture you want, click the Choose Picture button to select the image.

> ✓ **TIP** If you prefer a solid color background to a picture, click the Background drop-down list and choose Solid Color before making a background selection.

Customize the Lock Screen

The Lock Screen appears whenever your computer goes to sleep. When you want to wake up your computer and begin using it again, you see the Lock Screen image, which you then click to display a sign-in screen to access Windows 10. You can choose what type of background image appears on the Lock Screen: Windows Spotlight, which shows images from the Bing search engine; a Microsoft provided picture; or a slide show of images from your Picture folder or Windows Spotlight.

Choose a new Lock Screen background

1 In Settings, choose Personalization, and then click Lock Screen.

2 Click the Background drop-down list.

3 Click Picture.

4 In the Choose Your Picture section, click an image.

<svg>TIP</svg> **TIP**   You can affect what images are shown if you select Windows Spotlight for Lock Screen Images in step 3. With the Lock Screen displayed, in the top-right corner, move your pointer over Like What You See?, and then click either I Like It! or Not a Fan? to cast your vote. The next time you go to Spotlight, you'll see images more like those that you've endorsed. Spotlight can also learn about you and the services and features you use in Windows 10 to make suggestions on the Lock Screen about other features or apps that you might enjoy.

Adjusting colors and transparency

The colors that appear on various elements of your screen (for example, the taskbar and open window borders) have two functions. First, they might appeal to your personal color sense and make your computing environment more attractive. Second, they might make the content on the screen easier to see. You can configure Windows 10 to pick a color scheme that matches the background image you've chosen for your desktop or make the Start menu transparent. You can also choose from among several high-contrast color schemes which are especially helpful for those who have low vision. You can even customize and save high-contrast color themes to use the colors you prefer.

Control colors and transparency

1 In Settings, choose Personalization, and then click Colors.

2 Click the switch to turn on the Automatically Pick An Accent Color From My Background setting.

3 If you want the taskbar to change color (rather than remaining black), be sure the Show Color On Taskbar And Start Menu option is set to On.

4 Click to turn on or off the Make Start, Taskbar, And Action Center Transparent option.

5 Click High Contrast Settings to choose a color scheme in the Ease Of Access settings.

(continued on next page)

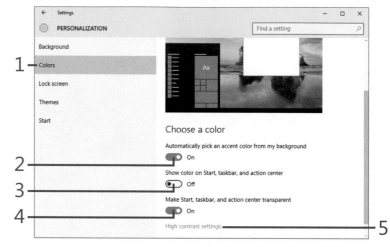

Control colors and transparency *(continued)*

6 Click the drop-down list at the top to display available themes.

7 Click a theme.

8 To customize your own theme, click any screen element, and then, from the palette that opens, choose a color.

9 Click Apply.

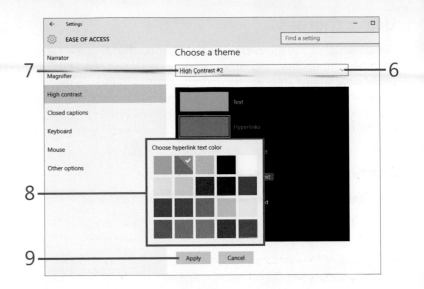

Using themes

Windows 10 includes several themes that control the appearance of your screen. These themes provide an easy way to apply a variety of settings such as colors, font, and background images to the computer interface. There are even high-contrast themes that make the screen easier to see for those who have low vision.

Select a theme

1 In Settings, choose Personalization, and then click Themes.

2 In the Themes section, click Theme Settings.

3 Click a theme to select it.

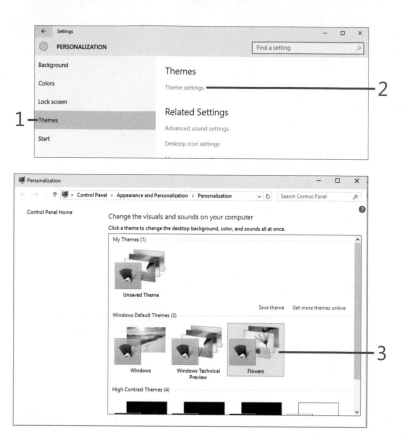

> **TIP** You can create your own themes. Before going to the theme window make any personalization settings you prefer. Then, in the theme window, click Save Theme. This opens a dialog box in which you can provide a name for your theme and save all current settings as a custom theme.

Changing the screen saver

You can set up a screen saver that will appear after a preset interval of inactivity on your computer. The screen saver is an animation that takes up the computer's full screen. A screen saver keeps your screen's contents private. When you want to get back to using your computer, you don't need to raise the Lock Screen and type your password or PIN; instead you can just click your mouse and your computer returns to whatever you were working on at the moment the screen saver activated.

Select a screen saver

1 In the Cortana search box, type **screen saver**.

2 Click Turn Screen Saver On Or Off.

3 Click the Screen Saver drop-down list, and then select a screen saver.

4 Click the up or down arrows on the Wait box (or you can also simply type a number directly in the box) to set an interval of inactivity after which the screen saver turns on.

5 Click Apply.

6 Click OK to close the dialog box.

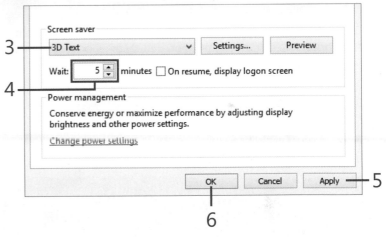

 TIP You can see what the screen saver will look like by clicking the Preview button in the Screen Saver Settings dialog box. The screen saver animation appears full screen. To return to the dialog box, press the Esc button on your keyboard.

Making timeout settings

After a certain interval of inactivity, Windows will go to sleep. When your computer is asleep you must click the Lock Screen and then type a password or PIN on the sign-in screen that opens to access your computer. You might find it disruptive if this happens after a very short interval. Conversely, if Windows waits a long time before it goes to sleep, you might end up draining your laptop battery of power unnecessarily.

You can control how quickly your computer goes to sleep or turns off when it's running on battery power or plugged into

a power outlet. Another way in which you can conserve power is by turning your screen off while still leaving the computer on. Although this doesn't save as much energy as when the computer goes to sleep, one benefit of turning off the screen is that it doesn't stop existing apps such as Music from working, whereas putting your computer to sleep stops apps from running and requires you to sign in again.

Choose when your screen times out

1 In Settings, choose Personalization, and then click Lock Screen.

2 Scroll down and click Screen Timeout Settings.

3 Click a drop-down list to choose a time interval for when the screen turns off while running on battery or when plugged in.

4 Click a drop-down list to choose a time interval for when the computer goes to sleep while running on battery or when plugged in.

5 Click the Close button.

> ⚠️ **CAUTION** Setting up too long an interval before your computer turns off the screen or goes to sleep can drain a laptop battery. Default settings are often suitable for most people, but if you do choose a lengthier interval, you should be aware of your power consumption trade-offs.

Enlarging text

If you want Windows interface text to be displayed in a larger size to help you read things more easily, you can use a System setting to choose the appropriate size. This setting doesn't control text size in apps, however. What it does control is text in Windows elements: dialog boxes, Settings windows, the taskbar, Start menu, and so forth.

Make text larger

1 In Settings, choose System, and then click Display.

2 Drag the slider for the Change The Size Of Text, Apps, And Other Items setting to the size you desire.

3 Click Apply.

TRY THIS If you have a touchscreen computer, you can also use your fingers to expand or reduce the display of many apps, including the Microsoft Edge browser. To enlarge the display, simply put two fingers together on the screen and spread them apart. To reduce the size of the display, place your fingers apart and pinch them toward each other.

TIP The Magnifier Ease of Access feature zooms in on areas of your screen to help those who have low vision see the screen as if they were holding a magnifying glass to it. See "Using Magnifier" on page 88 for more about using this feature.

Changing screen resolution

The monitor on your computer or laptop displays your desktop and its contents at a certain resolution, expressed in pixels in a ratio of height to width, such as 1024 x 768. Resolutions containing higher numbers provide a crisper screen, though elements might be smaller. Resolutions with a lower number provide a less crisp image, but elements are bigger, which might make the screen more readable for some. If you ever share images of your desktop you might be asked to shoot those images at a certain resolution, so it's useful to know how to change this setting.

Choose a screen resolution

1 In Settings, choose System, and then click Display.

2 Click Advanced Display Settings.

3 Click the Resolution drop-down list, and then select the setting you want.

4 Click Apply.

TIP Not all computers offer the same resolution options, because these depend on their screen quality. Newer computers with higher-quality displays and better-quality graphics cards will typically offer higher resolution settings.

Customizing the taskbar

You can customize the taskbar that runs along the bottom of the Windows desktop in several ways. First, you can control whether the taskbar is locked in place so that it can't shift to a different position (such as to the top, left, or right of your desktop). You can also control whether your taskbar is automatically hidden so that you can view the full screen without it until you move your pointing device near its position on the screen. You can move the taskbar to the top, bottom, right, or left of the screen. You can also change which Quick Action buttons, such as those that control volume, power, network connections, and so forth, appear on the right side of the taskbar.

Choose taskbar settings

1   Right-click the taskbar.

2   Click Properties.

3   Select any of the check boxes, such as Lock The Taskbar or Auto-Hide The Taskbar, to apply that setting.

4   Click the Taskbar Location On Screen drop-down box.

5   Click a location.

6   Click Customize for the Notification Area.

7   Click a Quick Action icon, and then, from the list that appears, select a different one.

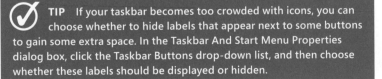

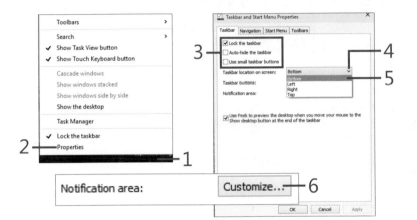

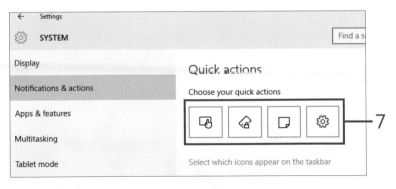

> **TIP**   If your taskbar becomes too crowded with icons, you can choose whether to hide labels that appear next to some buttons to gain some extra space. In the Taskbar And Start Menu Properties dialog box, click the Taskbar Buttons drop-down list, and then choose whether these labels should be displayed or hidden.

Adding tiles to the Start menu

There are several apps tiles included in the Start menu when you first turn on your Windows 10 computer. In designing Windows 10, Microsoft bet that these would be the most commonly used and useful tiles, but you can also choose which apps you prefer to pin to the Start menu.

Add a new tile to the Start menu

1 Click the Start button.

2 Click All Apps.

3 Right-click an app in the list.

4 Click Pin To Start.

> **⊘ TIP** Don't need an app on your Start menu anymore? You can remove an app tile by right-clicking it in the Start menu, and then, in the shortcut menu that opens, click Unpin From Start.

Moving tiles

The position of a tile on your Start menu can make it easier to find. For example, you might want to place your most commonly used app tiles along the top, and less-used tiles at the bottom. Or, you might decide to move a tile from one group of tiles to another. You can easily move tiles around on the Start menu by dragging them from place to place.

Move a tile

1 Click the Start button.

2 Drag a tile to a new location on the Start menu.

3 Release the mouse button.

 TRY THIS When you add tiles to the Start menu, they appear in a new group. Add a couple of tiles and then click above them and type a name for the new group. Try moving a tile from one group to another using the procedure described here.

Using Snap to arrange apps on the desktop

Snap is a feature that has been around for several versions of Windows. Snap helps you to quickly arrange open windows on the right or left side of your screen. In Windows 10 a vertical snap functionality has been added which makes it possible for you to move an open but not maximized app window to the top or bottom of your screen. The Snap feature works by selecting an app and dragging it, by using shortcut keys, or, with a touchscreen, by swiping an open app with your finger.

Snap apps

1 Using the Start menu, open several apps on the desktop.

2 Click an open app and quickly drag it to the left side of the screen.

(continued on next page)

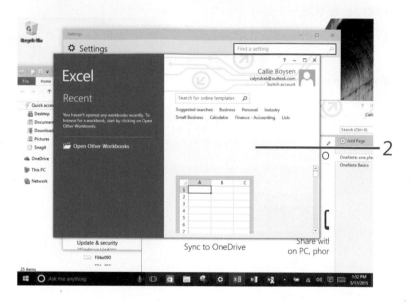

Snap apps *(continued)*

3 Click another app to expand it, and it opens on the right side of the screen.

4 Press the Windows logo key+Up arrow on your keyboard to snap a selected app to the top quadrant of the desktop.

5 Press the Windows logo key+Down arrow on your keyboard to snap a selected app to the bottom quadrant of the desktop.

> ✅ **TIP** If you have a touchscreen, note that dragging an open app's title bar to the top of the screen maximizes the app. Instead use the Windows logo key+Up arrow method described here.

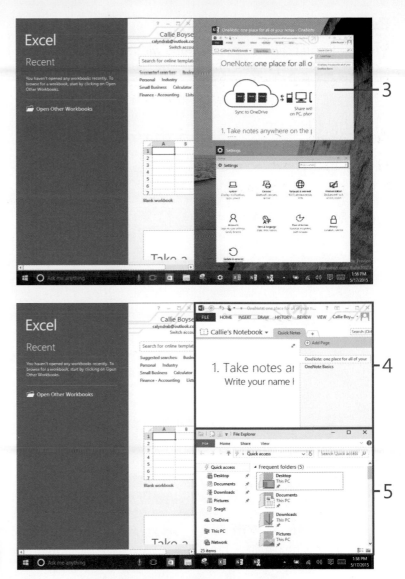

Resizing tiles

Your Start menu can become crowded with tiles as you continue to add apps to it. One way to relieve the clutter and view more tiles in the menu is to reduce the size of some tiles. You might also want to enlarge a tile that you want to more easily find. There are four sizes for tiles: Small, Medium, Wide, and Large. By default tiles appear in the Medium or Wide size.

Change tile size

1 Click the Start button.

2 Right-click a tile.

3 Click Resize

4 Click Small, Medium, Wide, or Large.

Working with productivity applications

These days, there is an app for just about anything, but many of these are small programs with limited functionality, such as a to-do list or calculator app. More robust applications (often used in a business setting, such as a word processor or database) incorporate more complex functionality. For example, you might work with text, numbers, images, and the ability to produce a graph, report, or slide show in a single application.

These full-featured products are called *productivity applications*. When you open such an application, you find that many share certain features, such as the ability to format text in several ways and to cut, copy, and paste items from one document to another or one location in a document to another. You complete many actions in productivity software by using a combination of toolbars and menus. When you finish creating a document, you can save it, print it, or share it. You might use these applications in the cloud, as with Microsoft Office 365, or they might be installed on your computer. Knowing how to use some basic functionality of productivity applications in Windows 10 will help you to get up to speed when you encounter a new application.

In this section:

- Finding and opening applications by using the Start menu
- Opening applications by using Cortana
- Working with toolbars and menus
- Cutting, copying, and pasting content
- Formatting text
- Formatting paragraphs
- Saving files
- Printing documents
- Sharing files via email
- Closing applications
- Uninstalling applications

Finding and opening applications by using the Start menu

The best way to find and open applications in Windows 10 is by using the Start menu. This menu offers a choice among the applications you use most, a list of all installed applications, and tiles that provide a visual way to access applications. Those tiles can be *live*—meaning that they show updated content from the Internet, as with a news or weather app—or they can be *static*—as with the People app.

Open an application by using the Start menu

1 Click the Start button.

2 Click All Apps.

3 In the All Apps list, scroll down (if necessary) and click an application to open it.

4 Click the Start button.

5 Click the Weather tile.

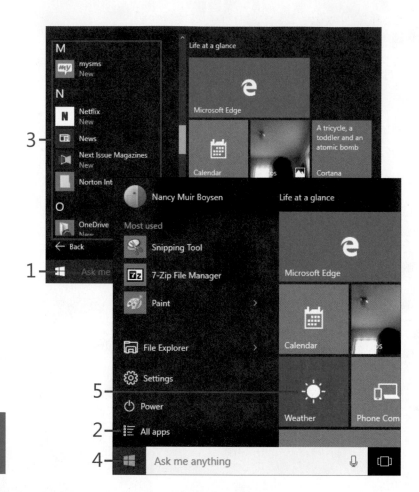

> **TIP**   Note that in the lower-left corner of the Start menu there are also links to File Explorer, Settings, and Power that you can use to access these frequently used features.

Opening applications using Cortana

You can use Cortana beyond just searching for information. She also performs certain actions on command, such as playing music or setting up a reminder. One useful feature of Cortana is her ability to open applications. You can ask Cortana to open an application just by asking her, or, in the Cortana search box, you can type **open** followed by the application name.

Ask Cortana to open an application

1 Click the Cortana search box.

2 Type the phrase **Open WordPad**.

3 Press Enter on your keyboard.

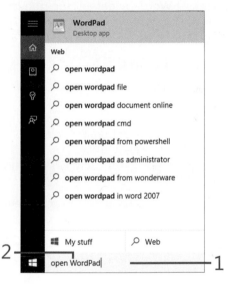

> ✓ **TIP** You can also click the microphone button in Cortana's search box and speak a phrase like the one in step 2 to open an app.

Working with toolbars and menus

A common element to most productivity applications is the use of tools and menus. Tools are icons arranged on a toolbar or, in the case of Microsoft productivity applications, a *ribbon*. Toolbars often include tabs that you click to display a different set of tools. For example, in Microsoft Word, by default the ribbon includes Home, Insert, Design, and Page Layout tabs, among others. These tabs break the tools into logical groups to help you find what you need. Productivity applications often also use menus with drop-down lists of commands that you can choose. In Word, to the left of the toolbar tabs, there is a File menu that presents commands such as Save and Print.

Use tools and menu commands

1 Open WordPad (see the previous task).

2 On the ribbon, click the View tab.

3 Clear the Ruler check box to remove the ruler from the screen.

4 Click the File menu.

5 Click Page Setup.

6 Click the Landscape button.

7 Click OK.

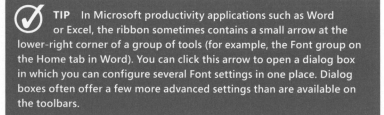

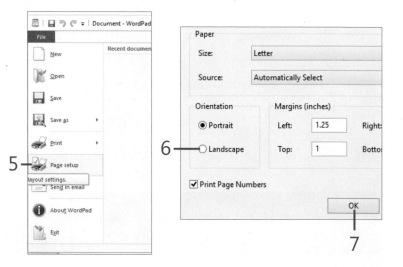

> **TIP** In Microsoft productivity applications such as Word or Excel, the ribbon sometimes contains a small arrow at the lower-right corner of a group of tools (for example, the Font group on the Home tab in Word). You can click this arrow to open a dialog box in which you can configure several Font settings in one place. Dialog boxes often offer a few more advanced settings than are available on the toolbars.

Cutting, copying, and pasting content

One useful function you'll find in productivity and other applications is the ability to cut, copy, and paste text and objects. You can perform these actions within a single document, or you can cut or copy content in one document and paste it into another. Cut removes content from the original location, whereas Copy makes a duplicate of the content but leaves the original in place. The Cut, Copy, and Paste tools make use of the Windows Clipboard, which is a holding place for cut or copied content.

Cut, copy, and paste

1 With WordPad open, type a sentence.

2 Drag your mouse pointer across the sentence to select it.

3 On the ribbon, on the Home tab, click the Cut or Copy button.

4 Click at the end of the original sentence, and then press Enter.

5 On the ribbon, click the Paste button.

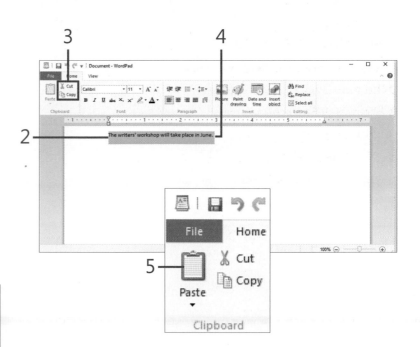

> ✓ **TIP** When you cut or copy something, it stays on the Clipboard until you cut or copy something else. You can paste the latest content of the Clipboard as many times as you like until it's replaced.

> ✓ **TIP** When you paste content, you might see a small icon at the end of the pasted item. Click this to choose paste options. For example, you might choose to retain the original formatting or apply the formatting in the new document to the pasted text.

Formatting text

Whether you're working in a database, a spreadsheet, a slide presentation application, or a word processor, it's likely that you'll add text to your document. You can format text in various ways; for example, by applying a different font, choosing a different color, or making the text bold or italic. Formatting text can make it look more appealing, professional, or even quirky, depending on the kind of document you're creating. You can use the Font tools in most applications to make formatting changes.

Apply formatting to text

1 With WordPad open, type this sentence: **We're experiencing unusually warm weather this year**.

2 Drag the mouse pointer to select the entire sentence.

3 On the ribbon, on the Home tab, click the Font drop-down list.

4 Click to select Book Antiqua.

5 Select the word **unusually**.

6 On the ribbon, click the Underline button.

7 Click the Text Color drop-down list, and then select a red color from the palette.

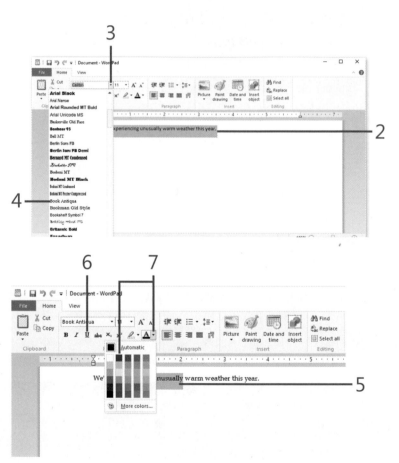

 TIP Some programs include sets of styles such as Normal, Heading 1, or Bullet List. These are part of the template on which you based your document. Styles usually contain several formatting settings such as the font and whether to add italic, making applying these groups of settings as simple as applying the style. Check your application's Help feature to see how to create and apply styles.

Formatting paragraphs

Many documents include sentences arranged in paragraphs. You can format paragraphs to add spacing between sentences within the paragraph and between the paragraphs themselves. You can indent the first line of a paragraph or the entire paragraph, as when citing a long quote. You can also align text in paragraphs to the left or right, or centered on the page. Finally, you can format a paragraph as a list with numbers or bullets.

Apply formatting to paragraphs

1 Open a document in WordPad or create a new document and type a paragraph.

2 Select the paragraph.

3 On the ribbon, on the Home tab, click the Line Spacing drop-down list, and then select 2.

4 Click the Increase Indent button.

5 Click the Start A List button.

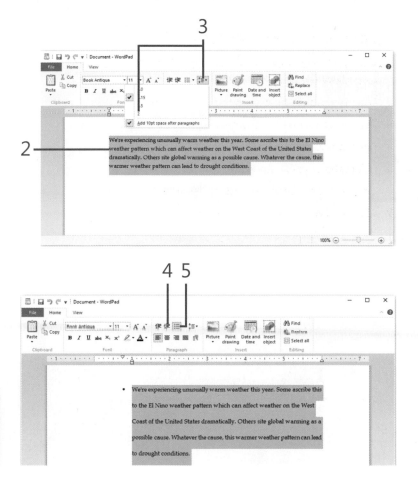

> **(→) TRY THIS** Many standard letter and report formats require that the first line of a paragraph be indented. On the WordPad ribbon, click the Paragraph button. In the dialog box that opens, click the First Line indentation box and increase the indentation to 1.

Saving files

By saving a document, you can continue working on it in the future or open it and review it or share it with others. When you save a document, you give it a name, and you can then open it from the originating application, or by locating it in File

Explorer. You can organize saved files in folders that you name in a way that makes items easier to locate at a later date. The first time you save a file, you'll use the Save command. If you want to save a file with a new name, use the Save As command.

Save a file

1 With a new document open in an application such as WordPad, click File.

2 Click Save.

3 On the left side of the Save As dialog box, click among the folders to find the location where you want to save the file.

4 In the File Name box, type a name.

5 If you want to save the file in a particular format, click the Save As Type drop-down list, and then select the format.

6 Click the Save button.

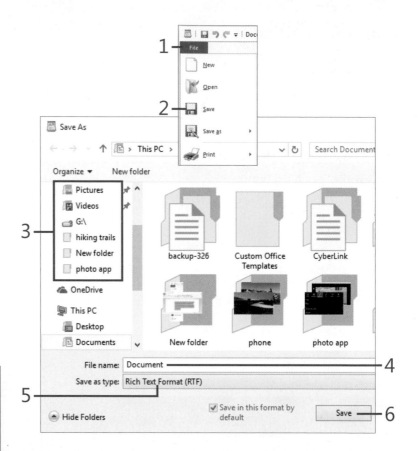

 TIP Don't wait until you're done working on a document to save it. If you don't save your changes every now and then while you're working, you risk losing the changes you've added. Though many applications have autosave features to save your files for you, to be absolutely sure, you should manually save your work every 5 or 10 minutes.

Printing documents

Although we live in a world that has been called "paperless," the fact is that we often need to print a hard copy of a document or image. Printing works pretty much the same way from one productivity application to another, though the choices might vary based on your printer model and manufacturer. For example, color options won't be available if your device prints only in black and white. Options commonly available include the number of copies; whether you want copies collated; orientation and size of the paper; whether to print in black and white, color, or grayscale; which range of pages in the document to print; and so on.

Print a document

1 With a document open in an application such as WordPad, click File.

2 Click Print.

3 In the list that displays on the right, click Print.

4 Select the printer to which you want to send your pages.

5 Select the number of copies.

6 Select the range of pages to print.

7 Click Print.

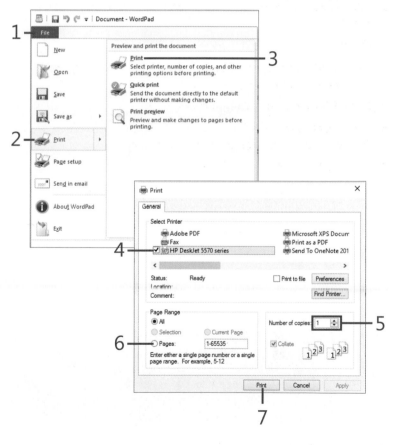

> **TIP** A shortcut to open the Print dialog box is to press Ctrl+P on your keyboard. There are some instances when a formal Print command isn't easy to find (for example on some sites on the web). In those situations, knowing this shortcut can prove invaluable.

Sharing files via email

Today, via the Internet, there are several ways to share documents with others, from sending them by email to creating an online presentation. The options you're offered for sharing depend on the application you're using. For example, with Microsoft PowerPoint, you can publish slides as an online presentation, and with Word, you can post a document on a blog.

For all applications on a Windows computer, you can save files to Microsoft OneDrive, an online file-sharing service. WordPad has less sophisticated sharing features, but you can send a document via Outlook email (you need to have or set up an Outlook email account before performing these steps).

Share a document via email

1 With a WordPad document open, click File.

2 Click Send In Email.

3 In the To box, type an email address.

4 In the Subject box, type a topic.

5 Type a message.

6 Click Send.

> **TIP** To save a file to OneDrive, click the File menu, click Save As, and then browse to locate OneDrive on your computer. This saves a copy of the document to your local OneDrive folder, which synchronizes periodically with the online OneDrive service. You can then share those documents with others from OneDrive.

Closing applications

When you're done working with an application for a time, although you can leave it running, you might want to close it. With fewer applications running, you free up some of your computer's memory, which improves performance. Closing an application is an easy process.

Close an open application

1 With an application open, first save any open document.

2 Click the Close button.

1   2

Uninstalling applications

If you no longer need an application on your computer, you can uninstall it. However, if there's a chance that you might need the application again someday, be sure that you have it either on disk or you have a product key for downloading the application from the Internet.

Remove an application from your computer

1 Click the Start button.

2 Click Settings.

3 Click System.

4 Click Apps & Features.

5 Click a program in the list.

6 Click the Uninstall button.

If you are prompted to give permission to make changes, type your account password, and then click Yes.

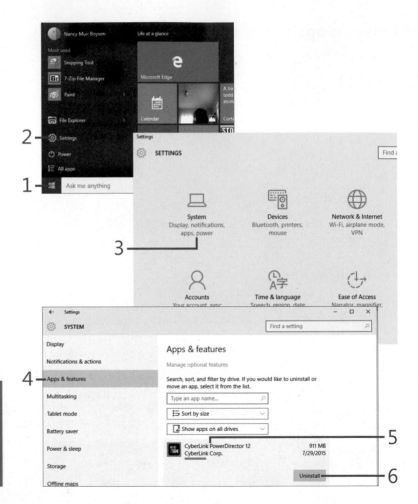

> ✓ **TIP** Depending on the application you're uninstalling, it might simply uninstall at this point, or Windows might ask you to confirm whether to uninstall by clicking a button labeled Finish or something similar. Some application suites—such as Office, which contains several applications—might ask you to choose which application to remove. Just respond to any prompts to finish the uninstall process.

Finding content with File Explorer and Cortana

File Explorer is the feature of Windows with which you can locate and organize the files saved on your computer and on external media such as USB sticks or DVD drives. File Explorer organizes content by using a hierarchy of files saved within folders and subfolders.

In addition, you can use the new personal assistant, Cortana, to find files and folders on your computer as well as information and content stored online. Using these two features of Windows, you can locate everything, from a single file saved on your computer to the virtually infinite content available on the Internet.

Finding content by using File Explorer

When you save files in Windows, you can create folders and place files within those folders to organize the files. File Explorer is like a table of contents for your computer's contents. When you open File Explorer, you can choose a drive, such as your computer's hard disk or a USB stick, move through its contents by selecting a folder—perhaps a subfolder—and then individual files. You can view a variety of information about files, such as the date they were last updated, their author, or their file size, by using File Explorer.

Locate files and folders

1 On the taskbar, click the File Explorer icon.

2 In the left panel, double-click a folder.

3 Double-click a subfolder if one exists.

4 Double-click a file to open it.

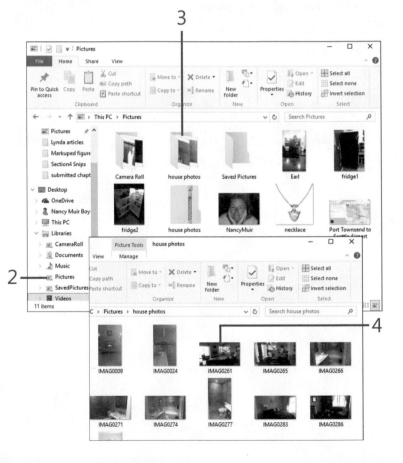

> **TRY THIS** You can use the Search feature in File Explorer to locate a file. With File Explorer open, click the Search box, and then type a file or folder name. Double-click an item in the results to open it.

Changing File Explorer views

People like to view information in different ways or with different levels of detail. In File Explorer you can choose to see a list of files and folders or icons of various sizes that represent the items. You can also choose to view a preview of a selected file or details about it such as its author, size, and the last date and time it was modified and saved.

Change views

1 On the taskbar, click the File Explorer icon.

2 Double-click a folder such as Pictures to open it.

3 On the ribbon, click the View tab.

4 In the Layout group, click List.

5 In the Panes group, click Details Pane.

6 Click a file to display its details in the right pane.

7 In the Panes group, click Preview Pane.

8 In the Layout group, click Medium Icons.

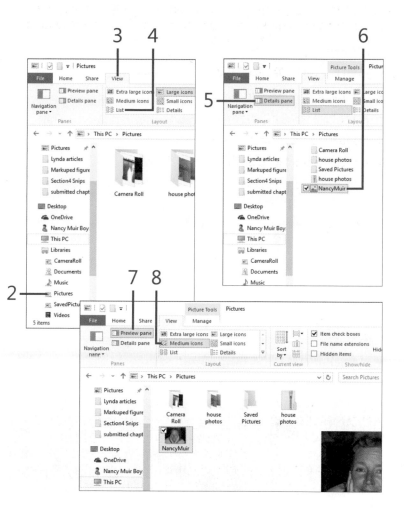

> **TIP** You can use the Show/Hide check boxes toward the right side of the View tab on the ribbon to show or hide elements or information such as check boxes to the left of files and folders in a list, file name extensions (such as .exe), hidden items, or items you've selected.

Sorting files

Being able to sort files by various criteria can help you to spot the file you need. For example, if you have a file named Vacation-March and another named Vacation-Islands that contain similar information, you might want to find the latest saved version or the one that's of a certain file type. With File Explorer, you can sort files by several criteria to help you locate just what you need.

Sort files

1 With File Explorer open, double-click a folder to open it.

2 Click a file and then, on the ribbon, on the View tab, click Details Pane.

3 Click Sort By.

4 Click to select a criteria such as Date or Size.

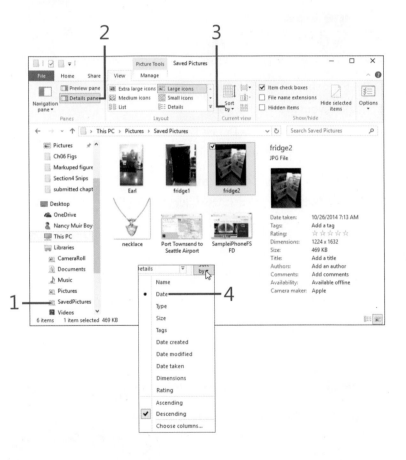

> ✓ **TIP** To sort files alphabetically, on the Sort By menu, choose the Ascending (A-Z) or Descending (Z-A) option.

> → **TRY THIS** If you want to have access to even more criteria, such as Album for Music or Postal Code for files named after addresses, in the Sort By drop-down list, click Choose Columns to display a list of additional options. Select a check box to choose one, and then click OK.

Creating a new folder

Folders are the way to organize your files in Windows, just as you place papers related to a particular project in a physical folder. You can use some folders that Windows provides out of the box, such as Documents and Pictures, or you can create your own folders. You can also create subfolders; for example, a construction project folder might contain subfolders for cost quotes, building plans, and correspondences.

Create a new folder

1 With File Explorer open, click the folder within which you want to create the new folder.

For example, you could click the Documents folder to create a subfolder within it.

2 On the ribbon, click the Home tab.

3 Click New Folder.

4 Type a name for the new folder.

5 Click anywhere outside the new folder to save the new name.

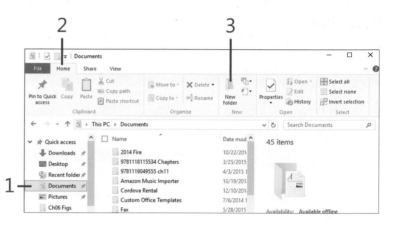

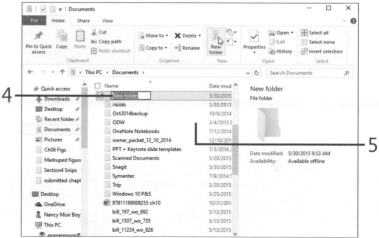

> **TIP** You can always rename a folder after you create it. See "Renaming files and folders" later in this section to find out how.

Moving files among folders

There are times when you might choose to move a file from one folder to another. Or, perhaps you want to place a copy of a file in another folder. For example, you might have a file containing a local caterer's menu that you keep in a restaurant menus folder, but you also want to place a copy in your daughter's wedding plans in that folder. You can either move a file from one location to another using the Cut button or make a copy of it by using the Copy button to have it available in both locations.

Move or copy one file to another location

1 With File Explorer open, locate a file to move or copy.

2 Click to select the file.

3 On the ribbon, on the Home tab, click Copy or Cut.

4 In the left pane, locate the folder to which you want to move or copy the file and double-click it.

5 Click the Paste button.

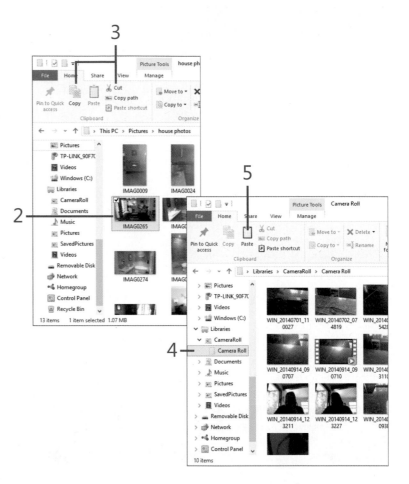

> **TIP** You can also drag a file or folder from one displayed folder to another folder in the left pane of the File Explorer window. However, be aware that this moves the file or folder to the new location, removing it from the original location.

Renaming files and folders

We tend to name files and folders on the fly, not always thinking of the most appropriate name. Occasionally, you'll want to rename a file or folder more accurately so that you can find it more easily or to differentiate it from another item. You can rename files and folders as many times as you like.

Rename a file or folder

1 In File Explorer, locate a file or folder.

2 Right-click the item.

3 On the shortcut menu that opens, click Rename.

4 In the text box that opens, type a name for the folder.

5 Click anywhere outside the text box to save the new name.

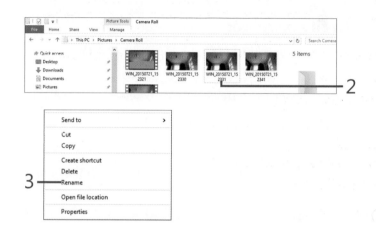

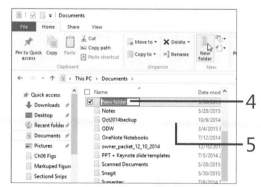

> ⚠️ **CAUTION** In Windows, you can name two folders in the same location with the same name, so be careful in renaming a folder that you don't duplicate a name, which could cause some confusion. Windows will not, however, allow you to name two files of the same type in the same folder using the same name. Instead, it will inform you that there's another file by that name, add "(2)" to the end of the name, and ask if you want to use that name.

Deleting files and folders

When you've archived an older file or folder on a storage medium, or you simply no longer need the item, you can delete it. Deleting old files not only clears some space on your computer's storage device, but it also makes folders easier to navigate when using File Explorer.

Delete a file or folder

1 With File Explorer open, on the ribbon, click the Home tab.

2 Click the item.

3 On the ribbon, in the Organize group, click Delete.

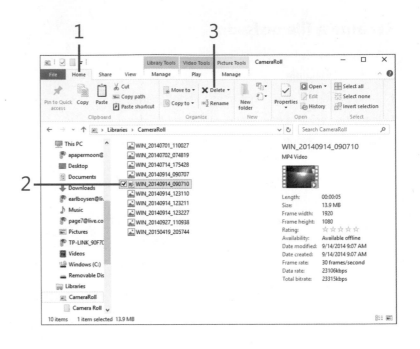

> ⚠ **CAUTION** Windows does not confirm the deletion of a file or folder, so be sure that you really want to delete it before clicking the Delete button. To be safe, if there's any chance that you might change your mind, back up the files on a USB stick or DVD before deleting them.

Compressing files

Although you can use an online sharing service such as OneDrive to store and share even large files easily, sometimes you might want to compress a file (also called *zipping*) to be able to attach it to an email or store it using less space. Compressing reduces the file size, making it easier to transmit to others who can then *unzip* the file on their computers.

Compress files into a zip folder

1 With File Explorer open, locate a series of files that you want to compress.

2 Click the first file, and then, while holding down the shift key on your keyboard, click the last file in the series.

3 On the ribbon, click the Share tab.

4 In the Send group, click Zip.

5 In the text box that opens, type a name for the compressed file.

6 Click anywhere outside the text box to save the name.

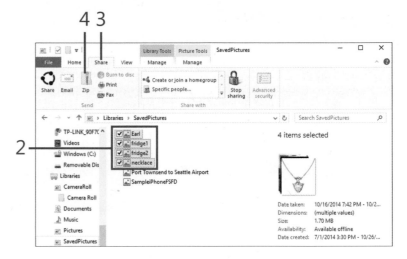

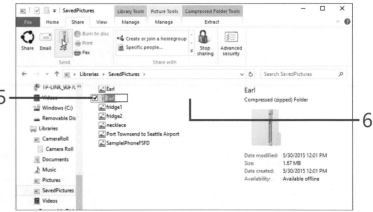

> **TIP** You should have all the files that you want to compress stored in the same folder on your computer. If the files are in the same folder but not adjacent to one another, click the first file, and then, with the Ctrl key pressed, continue to click additional files. When all of the files are selected, continue with step 3.

Sharing files via email

Who hasn't taken a picture or written an essay that they want to instantly share with others? Windows 10 offers many ways to share content, including by email, fax, and Fresh Paint (a photo editing program owned by Microsoft). File Explorer includes its own Share tab on the ribbon that offers you tools for sharing, emailing, printing, and faxing your content to others.

Send a file via email

1 With File Explorer open, locate and select a file that you want to share.

2 On the ribbon, click the Share tab.

3 In the Send group, click Email.

4 Fill out the Email form with an addressee, subject, and message.

5 Click Send.

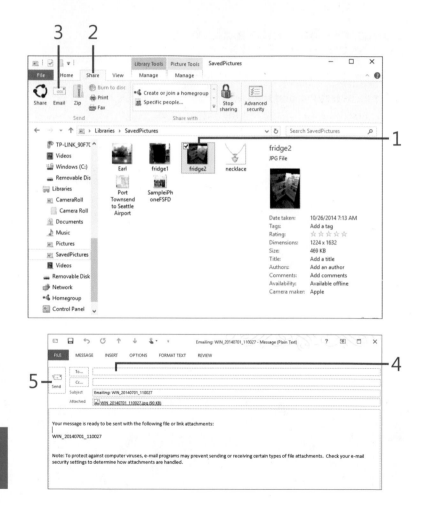

> **✓ TIP** To fax a file, you follow a similar process, except that you must connect to a fax modem first, and then fill out a fax form and send it with the attachment.

Searching by using Cortana

Cortana is touted as a personal assistant, and she can indeed perform a variety of actions. However, one of the main roles of Cortana is to act as a search tool, giving you the means to search both for items on your computer and items online. You can find Cortana on the taskbar, and she provides you with two ways to search: by voice command or by typing a search term using your keyboard.

Search by using Cortana

1 On the taskbar, click the Cortana search box.

2 Type a search word or phrase.

3 Click My Stuff to narrow your search results.

4 Click a result to open that file.

> ✓ **TIP** You can narrow your settings for files by typing a phrase such as Word files or Excel files before clicking My Stuff. You can also sort search results by criteria such as relevance to your search term or Most Recent to locate the most recently saved version of a file.

Searching for favorite places

You can use the Favorite Places feature of Cortana to search for and save locations such as nearby restaurants and movie theaters. Cortana searches for a list of favorites, and you can then save an item in your Favorites list so that you can access it easily in the future. Note that to achieve the most accurate results for local establishments, you should turn on the Location feature in the Action Center.

Find and add favorite places

1 Click in the Cortana search box.

2 Click the Notebook button.

3 Click About Me.

4 Click Edit Favorites.

5 Click the Add button.

(continued on next page)

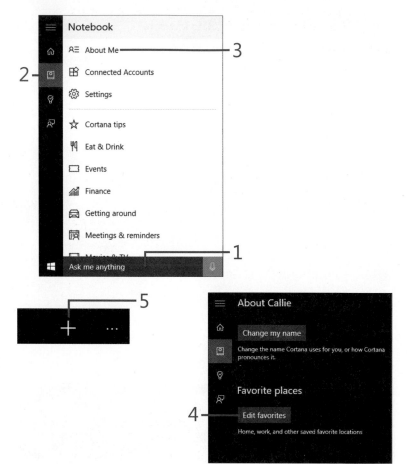

Find and add favorite places *(continued)*

6 In the Add A Favorite box, type a term.

7 Click a result.

8 Type a nickname, if you like.

9 Click the Set As Home or Set As Work settings to turn one on so that requests to Cortana for directions, weather, and so on can be answered based on the appropriate location.

10 Click Save.

 TIP To get a map to a location, open Favorite Places in Cortana, and then click Directions under a location. If asked, give permission for Cortana to access your current location. Cortana opens the Maps app and displays directions for you. For more about using the Maps app, see Section 19, "Using Maps."

Managing the Recycle Bin

When you delete a file or folder, it's sent to the Recycle Bin—a kind of trash can that holds your deleted content until it becomes so full that it destroys older contents. Even after you delete an item you can often use the Recycle Bin to locate

and restore it to your computer. The Recycle Bin is essentially a folder in File Explorer, which provides a Manage tab on the ribbon for managing Recycle Bin contents.

Restore an item from the Recycle Bin

1 From the desktop, double-click the Recycle Bin.

2 Click the Manage tab if it's not already displayed.

3 Click an item in the folder.

4 On the Ribbon, on the Manage tab, click Restore The Selected Items.

⊘ TIP To restore all items in the Recycle Bin, from the Recycle Bin window, on the Manage tab, in the restore group, click Restore All Items. You can also empty the Recycle Bin of all contents by clicking Empty Recycle Bin.

Making Windows accessible

Windows is used by millions of people around the globe. Some of those people face challenges in using a computer. Some have dexterity issues such as carpal tunnel syndrome or arthritis and need to adjust mouse and keyboard settings to make providing input easier. Others face visual challenges that make content on the screen difficult to read. Some might need help hearing sounds or require an alternative way to connect with the spoken word in videos, such as close captioning.

Windows 10 offers several accessibility features to address these needs, such as Magnifier to enlarge content on the screen, Narrator to read content to a user, the ability to adjust screen brightness or contrast, and the option of speaking text rather than typing it. All of these tools make using a Windows 10 computer very easy.

In this section:

- Using Magnifier
- Setting up high contrast
- Adjusting screen brightness
- Making elements on your screen easier to see
- Changing mouse settings
- Changing keyboard settings
- Using Touch Feedback
- Working with Narrator
- Using Speech Recognition
- Turning on Closed Captioning
- Using visual alternatives for sounds

Using Magnifier

Although it's possible to enlarge or reduce contents in many instances—such as on a webpage or in a word processed document—it's not possible to enlarge the Windows environment itself. For example, you can't enlarge the entire desktop (though you can enlarge the icons for desktop shortcuts). To enlarge your entire on-screen environment by a significant factor, you can use the Magnifier feature. This feature is useful to those who have low vision.

Turn on Magnifier

1 Click the Start button.

2 Click Settings.

3 Click Ease Of Access.

4 Click Magnifier.

5 Click to turn on Magnifier.

6 In the Magnifier controls, click the Zoom In button to zoom in.

7 Click the Zoom Out button to zoom out.

8 Click the Close button to close Magnifier.

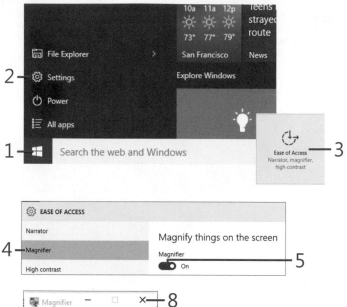

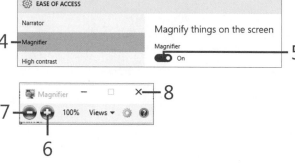

> **TRY THIS** For some people, a dark background with white text is easier to read. To invert color to make the screen black and text white, click Magnifier, turn on Magnifier, and then turn on Invert Colors.

> **TIP** If you have a touchscreen computer, you can also zoom in or out in Magnifier by pinching in or spreading out with two fingers on the screen.

> **TIP** After a few seconds, the Magnifier controls change to a magnifying glass icon. To redisplay the controls, click the magnifying glass.

Setting up high contrast

You can make elements on your screen easier to discern if you increase the contrast between lighter and darker colored objects. To do that, you can apply any of four preset high-contrast color schemes. These schemes control the color of your background, selected text, hyperlinks, and more.

Make high-contrast settings

1 In the Ease Of Access settings window, click High Contrast.

2 Click the Choose A Theme drop-down list.

3 Click a theme.

4 Click Apply

> **TIP** If you have difficulty discerning colors, choose a high-contrast theme that contains colors you can easily see.

Adjusting screen brightness

The brightness setting for your screen can make elements on the screen easier to see. However, be aware that if you're using a laptop, the brighter you set your screen, the quicker you'll drain your battery.

Set the screen to be brighter or dimmer

1 Click the Action Center button.

2 Click the Brightness button.

3 Click the button again to move to the next highest brightness level in increments of 25 percent.

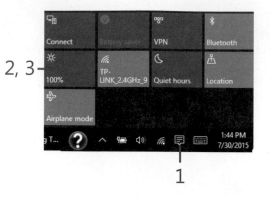

TIP You can also go to the System settings window and click Display to access a brightness slider. This slider gives you much greater control over the increments of brightness on your screen.

Making elements on your screen easier to see

You can adjust some visual options to help you spot certain elements on your screen. For example you can adjust the thickness of your mouse pointer (the little arrow on the screen that shows the location of your mouse). You can also control the duration for which notifications about your computer, such as how to handle a newly inserted USB stick, stay on the screen, to give you more time to read them.

Adjust how cursors and notifications appear

1 In the Ease Of Access window, click Other Options.

2 Click the Show Notifications For drop-down list and select an increment from 5 seconds to 5 minutes.

3 Click the Cursor Thickness slider and drag it to the desired width.

TIP   If it's easier for you to make out items on the desktop with no background showing, you can turn off the Show Windows Background setting in the Visual options window shown here. This turns your desktop background to black.

Changing mouse settings

Whether your mouse control comes from a touchpad or move-able mouse, when you use it around your screen, it displays a variety of symbols often called *pointers*. You can control the size and color of your mouse pointer in the Ease Of Access settings, and even configure it so that keys on your numeric keypad can control the movement of your pointer on the screen if you have trouble controlling a physical mouse device. When this feature is turned on, numeric keypads embedded in keyboards have keys that you can use to move the pointer up, down, left, and right, as well as paging up and down.

Change how your mouse works

1 In the Ease Of Access window, click Mouse.

2 Click to select a pointer size.

3 Click to select the pointer color (white, black, or white and black).

4 Click to turn the numeric keypad mouse control on or off.

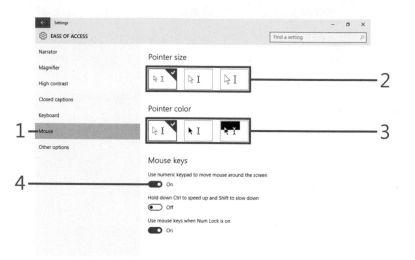

TIP When you turn on the numeric keypad to control the mouse, you can also use two other settings to press and hold the Ctrl key to speed up mouse functionality or use the mouse keys only when the Num Lock setting is set to on for your keyboard.

Changing keyboard settings

Using a keyboard can present certain challenges. If you have dexterity issues such as arthritis, pressing two shortcut keys at once can be difficult. In that case, you can use Sticky Keys to allow for pressing one key at a time when entering a shortcut on your keyboard. In addition, we've all pressed a key like Caps Lock without realizing it. In the Ease Of Access settings window you can turn on Toggle Keys, a feature that has your computer make a sound when you press Caps Lock, Num Lock, or Scroll Lock. Finally, Filter Keys is a feature that causes Windows 10 to disregard a brief or repeated key press. If you have dexterity challenges, this can be useful to avoid unintended entries.

Specify how you interact with your keyboard

1 In the Ease Of Access window, click Keyboard.

2 Click the switch to turn on Sticky Keys.

3 Click the switch to turn on Toggle Keys.

4 Click the switch to turn on Filter Keys.

TIP If you want to know if you've turned on or off a setting by pressing a shortcut key combination, in the Other Settings section, click the switches to turn on either (or both) Display A Warning Message When Turning A Setting On With A Shortcut or Make A Sound When Turning A Setting On Or Off With A Shortcut.

Using touch feedback

If you have a touchscreen computer, you will often touch the screen to select a feature or even to draw. Touch Feedback displays a pale circle when you touch the screen, providing you with visual feedback that your tap was recognized. You can turn Touch Feedback on or off and also turn on a setting to provide a more enhanced visual feedback indication on your screen.

Get feedback from your touchscreen

1 In the Ease Of Access window, click Other Options.

2 The Show Visual Feedback When I Touch The Screen setting is turned on by default. Click the switch to turn it on if the setting has been switched off.

3 Click the Use Darker, Larger Visual Feedback switch to turn it on.

TIP You must turn on the Show Visual Feedback When I Touch The Screen setting before you can access the setting to make the feedback darker.

Working with Narrator

If you have difficulty seeing what's on your screen, you might want to investigate the Narrator feature. Using Narrator, Windows can "speak," telling you what is currently displayed on the screen, describing items such as text and buttons. When you turn on the Narrator feature, you must click an element on the screen, such as an item in Settings to hear details about it, and then click it to activate it.

Turn on Narrator

1 In the Ease Of Access window, in the left pane, click Narrator.

2 Click the Narrator switch to turn on the feature.

3 Click the Start Narrator Automatically switch to turn on Narrator whenever you log in to Windows 10.

4 Click the drop-down list for Choose A Voice to select a male or female voice.

5 Click anywhere in the Speed setting to speed up the Narrator speech.

6 Click anywhere in the Pitch setting to adjust the pitch of the Narrator voice from lower to higher.

TIP You can configure additional Narrator settings in the Ease of Access, Narrator settings. For example, you can set which elements that you want Narrator to read, such as words you type and hints for buttons. You also have the option of highlighting mouse pointers, insertion points, and keys on a touch keyboard when you lift your finger from them.

Using Speech Recognition

Have you ever imagined spraining your wrist and not being able to use a keyboard to enter text in apps on your computer? Speech Recognition is a feature built in to Windows that you can use to provide speech input to your computer when you're using an application such as a word processor and then let your computer carry out entering the text you've spoken.

When you activate Speech Recognition, you need to ensure that your microphone is set up and that the app begins to learn your spoken patterns. When you've performed this basic setup procedure, you can then use this app to provide input to your computer.

Set up Speech Recognition

1 In the Cortana search box, type **Speech Recognition**.

2 In the results, click the Windows Speech Recognition Desktop App.

(continued on next page)

Set Up Speech Recognition (continued)

3 Click Next.

4 Choose the type of microphone that you will use, and then click Next.

5 Proceed through several more screens of the wizard to make settings choices.

⚠ **CAUTION** Speech recognition technology has come a long way since it was created, but it's still a technology that's evolving. When you dictate something using this feature, be sure to proofread it for any errors, which can range from your computer entering "to" when you meant "two," or missing a word in a sentence.

✓ **TIP** After you set up Speech Recognition, you can type the phrase *speech recognition* in the Cortana search box and then press Enter. Speech Recognition opens in Listening mode. Speak a command such as "Open Excel," or, if you have displayed a document, you can speak words, numbers, or punctuation that you want to enter. To close the feature, click the Close button (X) on the Speech Recognition controls that appears near the top of the screen, or the – symbol to minimize it.

← 🎙 Set up Speech Recognition

Welcome to Speech Recognition

Speech Recognition allows you to control your computer by voice.

Using only your voice, you can start programs, open menus, click buttons and other objects on the screen, dictate text into documents, and write and send e-mails. Just about everything you do with your keyboard and mouse can be done with only your voice.

First, you will set up this computer to recognize your voice.

Note: You will be able to control your computer by voice once you have completed this setup wizard.

3 — [Next] [Cancel]

← 🎙 Set up Speech Recognition

What type of microphone is Microphone (Realtek High Definition Audio)?

● **Headset Microphone**
Best suited for speech recognition, you wear this on your head.

○ **Desktop Microphone**
These microphones sit on the desk.

○ **Other**
Such as array microphones and microphones built into other devices.

4 — [Next] [Cancel]

Turning on closed captioning

If you are hard of hearing, you might have used the closed-captioning feature on a television so that you could read what's being said. Your Windows computer also has a closed captioning feature, and you can set up the color, transparency, font style, and size of the captions in the Ease Of Access settings window.

Choose closed captions options

1 In the Ease Of Access settings window, in the left pane, click Closed Captions.

2 Click to choose a Caption Color.

3 Click to choose whether to make the caption opaque, translucent, semitransparent, or transparent.

4 Click to choose a Caption Style for your font, such as serif, sans serif, or small caps.

5 Click to choose a size for your caption.

6 Click to choose Caption Effects such as a drop shadow or raised text.

> **TIP** You can see a preview of your choices in the Preview section of the Closed Captions setting. Some settings might make your captions harder to read against busy backgrounds, so you'll need to experiment.

Using visual alternatives for sounds

Windows uses sounds to notify you of different events such as critical battery alerts or calendar reminders. It sound feedback when you're interacting with Windows is difficult for you to hear, you might prefer visual indicators. You can choose to have Windows 10 flash the active title bar, active window, or the entire display in place of sounds.

Set up visual notifications for sounds

1 In the Ease Of Access settings window, in the left pane, click Other Options.

2 Click the Visual Notifications For Sound drop-down list.

3 Click one of the three notifications options in the list to turn one on.

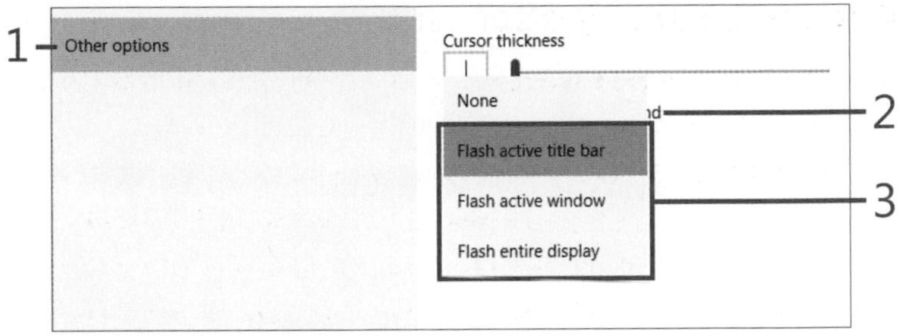

TIP To turn off visual notifications, in the drop-down list shown here, choose the selection None.

Accessing and managing networks

A computer network makes it possible for several computers to join and share resources such as an Internet connection or printer as well as documents. Using Windows 10, you can create a new network, join an existing network (including public networks such as those in restaurants and airports), and make settings for sharing. Your home network or a public network you access from a laptop or tablet computer as you travel around functions using a technology called *Wi-Fi*.

Beyond knowing how to join and access a network, it's important to be aware of security and privacy settings so that those outside the network can't access your content and settings information.

In this section:

- Understanding Wi-Fi networks
- Connecting to a network
- Joining a homegroup
- Managing Wi-Fi Sense settings
- Making your computer discoverable
- Setting file and printer sharing options
- Using Airplane Mode
- Disconnecting from a network

Understanding Wi-Fi networks

Wireless networks are everywhere. They provide an access point for computers to go online. Individuals need to connect to a network and provide a password. Networks can be public or private. Typically, a private network is secure, and, as such, only those who have joined the network can connect to it. You can find a public network in places such as a hotel, café, or library. These networks are open to anybody who gets the password from the network owner; they are, therefore, less secure.

and tablets can use the wireless signal from the wireless router to access the Internet connection and share resources.

If you have a home network, you need to have each computer in your network set up in the network *homegroup*, and you can grant permissions for those users to share content and functions such as an Internet connection. If there are peripherals such as a printer connected to the network, these also can be shared.

Understand how a Wi-Fi network works

A simple home network requires a piece of equipment called a *modem/router* connected to an incoming Internet connection through your provider (for instance, the cable or phone company). This modem/router is connected by a cable to a *wireless router*. Computers and other devices such as phones

> **TIP** If you want to connect a single computer to the Internet, you can use a modem/router and a cable plugged into a provider connection in your wall (typically phone or cable). You then use an Ethernet cable to connect your computer with the modem/router. With a single computer there's no need to broadcast the connection wirelessly to other computers (unless you want to use your single computer in multiple locations throughout your house), so no wireless router is required.

> **TIP** Virtually all computers today are Wi-Fi capable; however, if you have an older model that does not have Wi-Fi capability, you can buy a Wi-Fi adapter that plugs in to a USB port on your computer. You can also purchase a *Mi-Fi* (mobile wireless) hotspot with which you can connect your computer to your cellular connection.

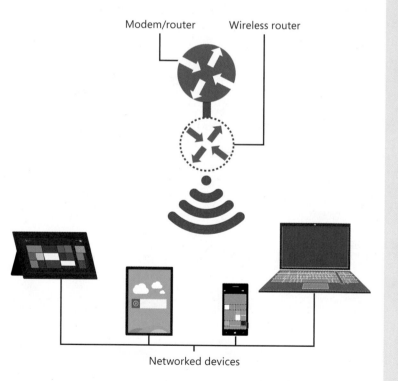

Modem/router   Wireless router

Networked devices

Connecting to a network

You need a few things in place to connect to a network. First, your computer must be Wi-Fi enabled, and Wi-Fi needs to be turned on in your Wi-Fi settings (you can simply click the Wi-Fi button in the Action Center to switch Wi-Fi on and off). Second, you need to be within range of the network; depending on the network strength, this could be up to approximately 300 feet. Finally, you need to select the network and provide a password. After you join a network for the first time, many networks allow you to sign in at any time without providing the password each time.

Connect to a network

1   On the taskbar, click the Network button.

2   From the list of available networks, select a network.

3   If you want to connect to this network every time you log in to Windows 10, select the Connect Automatically check box.

4   Click the Connect button.

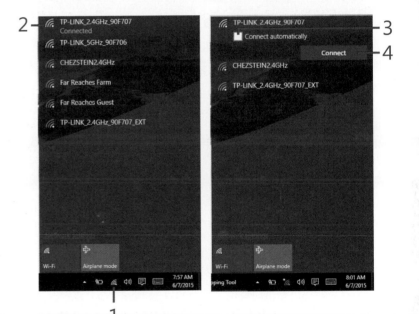

Joining a homegroup

On a home network, you set up a homegroup. Any computer that belongs to the homegroup can share things. They can easily share documents, printers, music, and videos with one another. You can control what you share with others (see "Setting file and printer sharing options" later in this section)

via Windows Settings. Joining a homegroup requires that you get the homegroup password from your network administrator; note that this is a different password from the one you use to connect with a network.

Join a homegroup on a home network

1 On the taskbar, right-click the Network button.

2 Click Open Network And Sharing Center.

3 Click HomeGroup.

4 Click the Join Now button, and then, in the following screen, click Next.

(continued on next page)

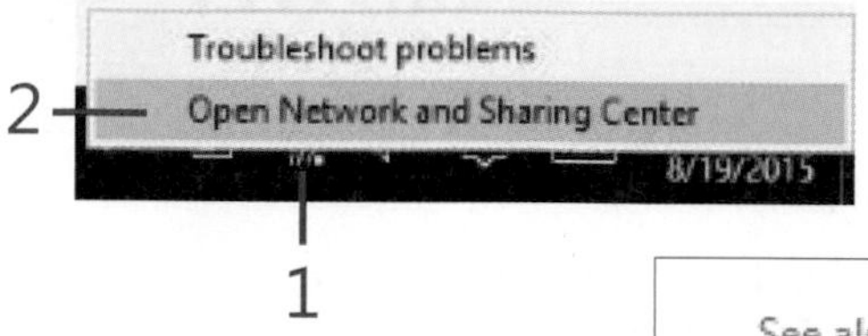

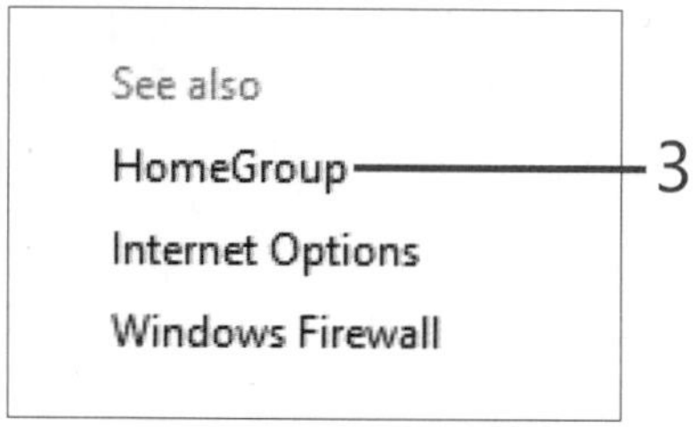

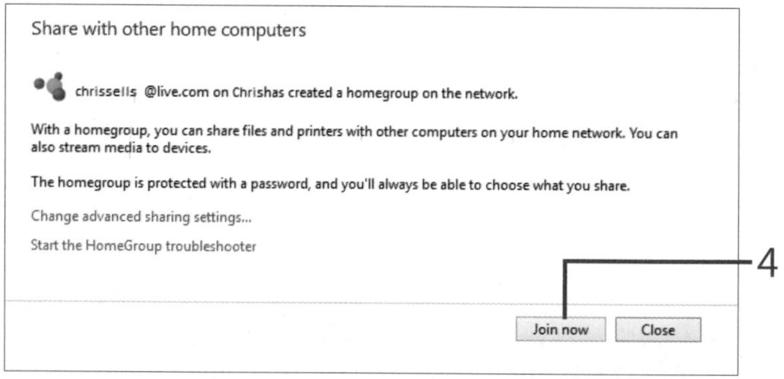

Troubleshoot problems

2 — Open Network and Sharing Center

8/19/2015

1

See also

HomeGroup ———— **3**

Internet Options

Windows Firewall

Share with other home computers

chrissells @live.com on Chrishas created a homegroup on the network.

With a homegroup, you can share files and printers with other computers on your home network. You can also stream media to devices.

The homegroup is protected with a password, and you'll always be able to choose what you share.

Change advanced sharing settings...

Start the HomeGroup troubleshooter

Join now   Close   **4**

Join a homegroup on a home network _(continued)_

5 Click an item to make it Shared or Not Shared.

6 Click Next.

7 Type your homegroup password.

8 Click Next.

9 Click Finish.

TIP To obtain the password for the homegroup, contact the person who created it, whose email is provided when you are using the homegroup wizard. That person can go to the homegroup settings to locate the password.

← 🖳 Join a Homegroup

Share with other homegroup members

Choose files and devices you want to share, and set permission levels.

Library or folder	Permissions
🖼 Pictures	Shared ⌄
▣ Videos	Shared ⌄
🎵 Music	Shared ⌄
🗎 Documents	Not shared ⌄
🖨 Printers & Devices	Shared ⌄

— 5

Next   Cancel

— 6

← 🖳 Join a Homegroup

Type the homegroup password

A password helps prevent unauthorized access to homegroup files and printers. You can get the password from jchrissells@live.com on Chrisor another member of the homegroup.

Type the password:

7 ——— [   ]

Finish — 9

Making Wi-Fi Sense settings

Wi-Fi Sense is a new feature in Windows 10 by which your computer can easily connect to Wi-Fi hotspots (public and private networks) and share them with your contacts. After you share a network using Wi-Fi Sense settings, you and your contacts can access the contents of the network without sharing a network password.

Make use of Wi-Fi Sense

1 In Settings, click Network & Internet.

2 Click Wi-Fi.

3 Click the Manage Wi-Fi Settings link.

(continued on next page)

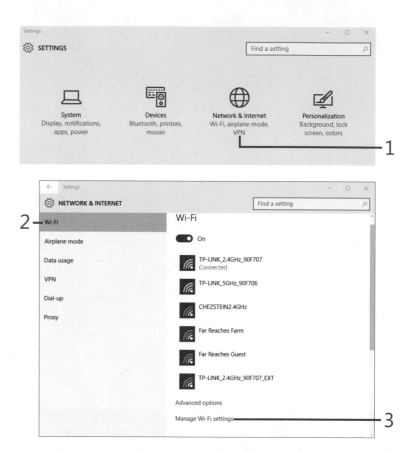

Make use of Wi-Fi Sense *(continued)*

4 Click the Connect To Networks Shared By My Contacts switch.

5 Click a network name.

6 Click Share.

4 ────● Settings / MANAGE WI-FI SETTINGS

Connect to suggested open hotspots — On

Connect to networks shared by my contacts — On

For networks I select, share them with my

☑ Outlook.com contacts

☑ Skype contacts

☑ Facebook friends

Wi-Fi Sense needs permission to use your Facebook account

Give and get Internet access without seeing shared passwords. You'll get connected to Wi-Fi networks your contacts share, and they'll get connected to networks you share.

Manage known networks

5 ──── Boysen
Not shared

6 ──── Share   Forget

> ⚠ **CAUTION**   If you use a shared network, be aware that it might not be secure. Avoid sharing financial information, logging in to your bank account or retail account, and so on when connected to such a network.

Making your computer discoverable

Bluetooth is a short-range wireless connection through which various devices can connect with one another. You might have paired your smartphone with your car or your computer to a printer via Bluetooth, for example. If you want your computer to be available for a Bluetooth pairing, you need to make it *discoverable* by other devices.

Make your computer discoverable on a network

1 In Settings, click Network & Internet.

2 Click Wi-Fi.

3 Click Advanced Options.

4 If the switch for the Find Devices And Content is set to off, click it to turn it on.

> **TIP** You can make your computer discoverable so that your smartphone can use your Wi-Fi network to go online rather than using its cellular network. This can save you data charges that you might otherwise incur when uploading or downloading data.

Setting file and printer sharing options

Most people find that sharing files and a printer with others on a network makes life easier. You don't need to send files by email or share them online, and you don't need to have every

computer on a home network physically connected to a printer. To turn on this functionality, you first need to configure File And Printer Sharing settings.

Configure Sharing settings

1 In the Network & Internet settings window, click Wi-Fi.

2 Click Change Advanced Sharing Settings.

3 Click Turn On File And Printer Sharing, if it's not already selected.

4 Click Save Changes.

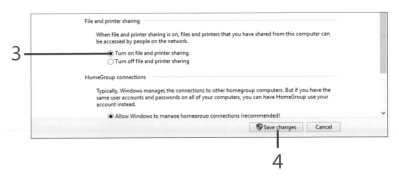

> ✓ **TIP** If you're finding that file and printer sharing isn't working, take a look at your Windows Firewall settings. You have the option to allow or not allow an app or feature to pass by the firewall. Select the printer and file sharing option to allow these sharing features to proceed.

Using Airplane Mode

When you're flying on an airplane, the flight crew usually requests that you turn off electronic equipment during takeoff or landing. With Windows 10, you can comply with this request while still being able to safely use your computer in flight by using Airplane Mode. Airplane Mode suspends all signal transmissions from Wi-Fi, Bluetooth, or a cellular connection so that they don't interfere with the plane's communications.

Turn on Airplane Mode

1 On the taskbar, click the Action Center button.

2 Click Airplane Mode.

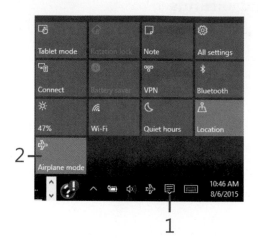

> ✓ **TIP** To turn off Airplane Mode, click the button in the Action Center again.

> ⚠ **CAUTION** With Airplane Mode turned on, you won't be able to send or receive email, or text or place calls using an Internet service such as Skype. As soon as you land and turn off Airplane Mode, however, you can retrieve any messages that have been sent while you were cruising the skies.

Disconnecting from a network

We often learn, usually quite by accident, that simply moving a distance away from a network will disconnect your computer. If, however, you want to disconnect from a network while still sitting within range of it—perhaps to avoid sharing or hacking by others—follow these simple steps.

Disconnect from your network

1 In the Network & Internet settings window, click Wi-Fi.

2 Click a network that is connected.

3 Click Disconnect.

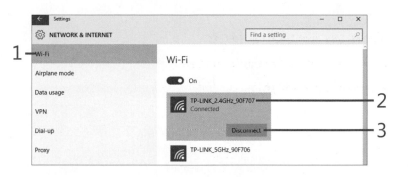

 TIP When you're connected to a public network your computer and the information it contains is always at risk. If you join a public network, when you're done using it, it's a good idea to disconnect from it.

Going online with Microsoft Edge

Microsoft Edge is a brand new browser that comes with Widows 10. Edge sports a cleaner, simpler interface than most other browsers, which helps users to concentrate on content rather than toolbars and menus. Within this interface, you can browse websites and search for content on webpages.

In addition to its sparser interface, Edge offers features to keep you secure when browsing, and to keep track of favorite websites and your browsing history. Using Reading View, you can display articles without the clutter of ads and unrelated pictures that appear on many webpages. In addition, you can draw on webpages and share them with others.

In this section:

- Getting an overview of Edge
- Setting a home page
- Browsing among webpages
- Working with tabs
- Viewing your browsing history
- Marking up webpages
- Using Reading View
- Adding items to Favorites or Reading List
- Using InPrivate browsing
- Finding content on pages
- Zooming in and out
- Managing downloads

Getting an overview of Edge

Edge brings with it a new look and feel for a browser. To keep the interface more clear from clutter, tools such as Favorites, Reading List, and History are accessed by using the Hub button. You can display a set of tools for marking up and sharing webpages by clicking the Make A Web Note button. Nesting these tools keeps the Edge toolbar uncluttered.

In addition to the simpler look, you can use the Web Note feature to draw on a webpage, insert typed comments, or highlight items, and then share that marked up page with others. Edge is also the browser used by the Windows 10 personal assistant, Cortana, making it possible for you to perform advanced web searches from your desktop.

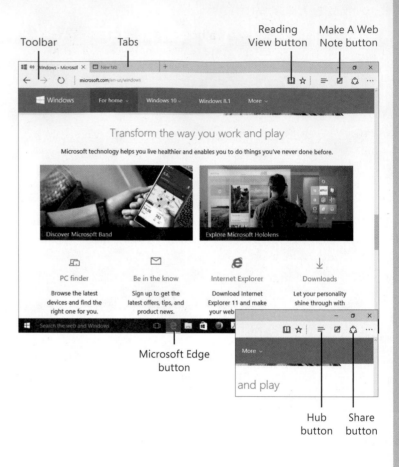

Toolbar   Tabs   Reading View button   Make A Web Note button

Microsoft Edge button

Hub button   Share button

TIP Because Edge is new, not every webpage opens in it. In some cases, a page will open in the Internet Explorer browser.

Setting a home page

When you open any browser, a home page appears. You can select the home page that Edge opens when you start it or click the Home button; in a sense, it acts as your home base for browsing the web. Perhaps you want a home page that displays current stock values or the weather, for example. You can set up more than one home page, and each will appear on its own tab.

Specify a home page

1 Open Edge and then, in the top-right corner of the window, click the More button.

2 Click Settings.

3 Click A Specific Page Or Pages.

4 Click the drop-down list beneath this setting and choose Custom.

5 In the Enter A Web Address box, type the address that you want to use as your home page.

6 Click the Add button.

> ✓ **TIP** To delete a home page, on the Settings panel, click the X directly to the right of the page name.

Browsing among webpages

The main function of a browser is, as the name implies, to browse the Internet, going from website to website or from one page in a website to another. Each location on the web is uniquely identified by a URL, such as *www.Microsoft.com*. With

Edge, you can use URLs to go to a particular site. You can also use the Back and Forward buttons to move back and forth between sites that you've just displayed in your current browsing session.

Move among webpages and sites

1 With Edge open, in the Address bar, type a URL for a website.

2 From the drop-down list, select the site that you want to visit, or press Enter.

3 Click the Back button to go to the previous page.

4 Click the Refresh button to reload the page.

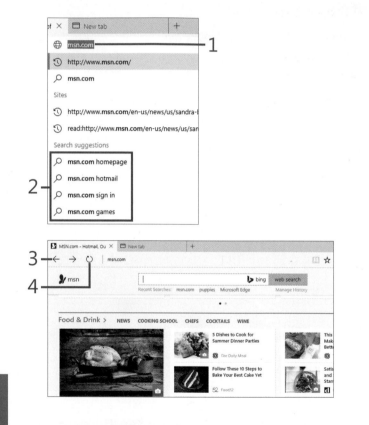

 TIP After you've moved among several webpages, you will have both the Back and Forward buttons available to you. The Back button takes you to the previously displayed page. The Forward button takes you to a website you've visited from the current page.

Working with tabs

By using tabs in browsers, you can have several sites open at one time and move among them by simply clicking a tab. For example, if you were researching a topic, the ability to move among tabs to crosscheck facts would be very useful. You can also keep a tab open so that you can quickly return to it after some time spent dealing with another task.

Open a new tab

1 With Edge open, click the New Tab button.

2 In the Where To Next? box, click a suggested site or type a URL, and then press Enter.

3 After you go to a site, the words New Tab are replaced by the site name.

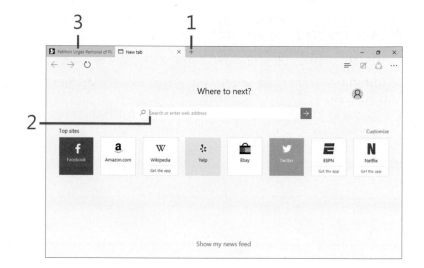

TIP To locate the URL of a site you've visited recently you can use the History feature, which is covered in the next task.

Viewing your browsing history

When you use a browser, you leave a trail of sites that you've visited. It's often handy to be able to look at that trail to find a site you want to revisit when you've forgotten its URL. Using the History tab, you can look at your browsing history and click a site to go there again.

See recently visited sites

1 With Edge open, click the Hub button.

2 Click the History tab.

3 Scroll down to view the sites you've visited.

4 Click the Last Hour setting and choose another timeframe for your history display.

TIP To remove your history of sites visited—perhaps to keep your activities private from others—on the History tab of the Hub, click Clear All History.

Marking up webpages

With Edge comes a new feature called Web Note. Using Web Note, you can turn on an editing mode in which you can write, draw, or insert typed comments on a webpage, and then share that markup with others or keep a record for yourself.

Draw on webpages

1   With a webpage open in Edge, click the Make A Web Note button.

2   Click the Pen tool and then draw on the page.

3   Click the Highlighter tool and then highlight some content on the page.

4   Click the Add A Typed Note button and then, in the box that appears, type a note.

5   Click the Share button.

6   Choose either Mail or OneNote, and then type requested information to share the marked-up page.

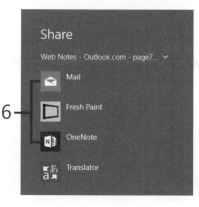

> **TIP**   You can also use the Share button outside of the Web Note editing mode to share any webpage you like via Mail or OneNote.

Using Reading View

With Reading View, you can remove the clutter of a webpage to present the content in a more magazine-like style. Reading View enlarges the text of an article slightly, as well, making it easier to read. You open Reading View by clicking the Reading View button, which is located on the Address bar. However, be aware that Reading View works only with websites that support this feature.

Open Reading View

1 With an article open on a webpage in Edge, click the Reading View button.

2 Click the Reading View button again to leave Reading View.

Adding items to Favorites or Reading List

As you browse the Internet, you might find articles or information that you want to read but can't take the time to read them right at that moment. In that case, you can save them to your Reading List and come back to read them at a later time.

Work with Favorites and Reading List

1 With a webpage open in Edge, click the Add To Favorites Or Reading List button.

2 Click either Favorites or Reading List.

3 Type a name for the item.

4 Click Add.

> **TIP** If you choose to add an item to Favorites, you can also choose to create the item in Favorites or the Favorites Bar, or even create a new folder to which to save the item.

Using InPrivate browsing

When you browse the Internet, you can leave your browsing history open to others' eyes or allow sites to place tracking cookies on your computer that identify you to others. InPrivate browsing is a feature with which you can browse in privacy, thereby keeping your online actions secure.

Keeping browsing data private

1 With Edge open, click the More button.

2 Click New InPrivate Window.

3 Type a URL and then press Enter to go to a website with InPrivate browsing active.

> ⚠️ **CAUTION** InPrivate browsing opens a tab that uses the feature; other tabs do not, so be careful to use an InPrivate tab for any browsing that you want to remain private.

Finding content on pages

A web browser is all about finding the information you need while you're online. Just as you might need to search to find content in a document, so might you also need to search for content on a webpage.

Search for content on a webpage

1 With Edge open, click the More button.

2 Click Find On Page.

3 In the Find On Page box, type your search text.

4 Click the Forward button to view the next result.

TIP To further refine your search, click Options, and then select Match Whole Word or Match Case.

Zooming in and out

One of the benefits of reading content online rather than in a book or magazine is that you can adjust the size of that content easily. You can zoom in to view larger text and pictures, or zoom out to fit more on your computer's screen—whatever accommodates your reading preference.

Enlarge or reduce a webpage

1 With a webpage open in Edge, click the More button.

2 To enlarge the view, in the Zoom control, click the Zoom In button.

3 Reduce the view, click the Zoom Out button.

TIP If you have a touchscreen computer, you can use your fingers to zoom in and out on a page. To zoom in, pinch your fingers together, place them on the screen, and then spread them outward. To zoom out, touch the screen with your fingers spread apart and then bring them together.

Managing downloads

Often while you're browsing online, you will come across items that you want to download, such as an app, a piece of music, or an image. When you do this, in most cases your content is downloaded to the Downloads folder on your computer, though you can choose to download it to other locations. Your download history is available to help you keep track of this content.

Manage your downloads

1 With Edge open, click the Hub button.

2 Click the Downloads tab.

3 Click the Open Folder button to open the Downloads folder on your computer.

TIP To clear your download history, in the Downloads panel, click the Clear All button. To pin a downloaded item to the Start menu, click the Pin button.

Connecting with others

10

Even in this hi-tech age, it's still true that our human contacts are often what matter most. In many cases, technology makes it possible for us to communicate with one another so that we can work on projects, share information, or connect with family or friends.

Windows 10 offers the People app that helps you to focus on connecting with others. In addition there are sharing features that Windows provides through which you can share a photo or document via email or social-networking services such as Twitter and Facebook.

In this section:

- Adding contacts in People
- Editing contacts
- Linking contacts
- Sharing contacts

Adding contacts in People

From new friends to new business acquaintances or new favorite restaurants, we gain more contacts all the time. People is a great centralized place to keep that information. You can copy contacts from your Microsoft email accounts to save you time, and add copies, one by one, from within the People app itself. If you include an address for a contact, a link is added that you can use to display that address in the Maps app.

Add a contact

1 Click the Start button.

2 Click the People app tile.

If the tile isn't visible, click All Apps, and then, in the All Apps list, click People.

(continued on next page)

Add a contact *(continued)*

3 Click the Add button.

4 Click a text box to add information such as Name, Mobile Phone, or Personal Email.

5 Click Save.

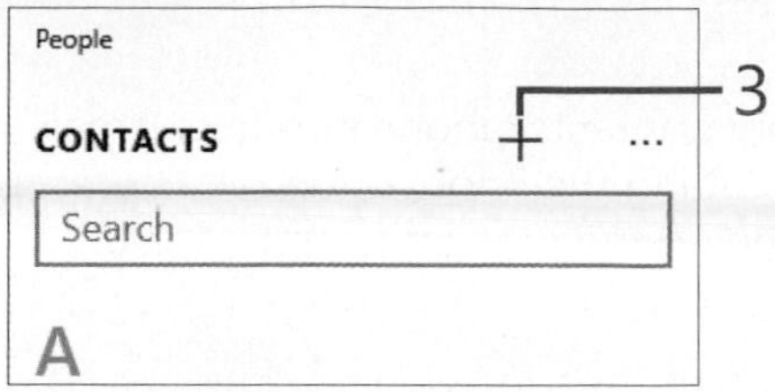

People

CONTACTS   +   ...   ─3

Search

A

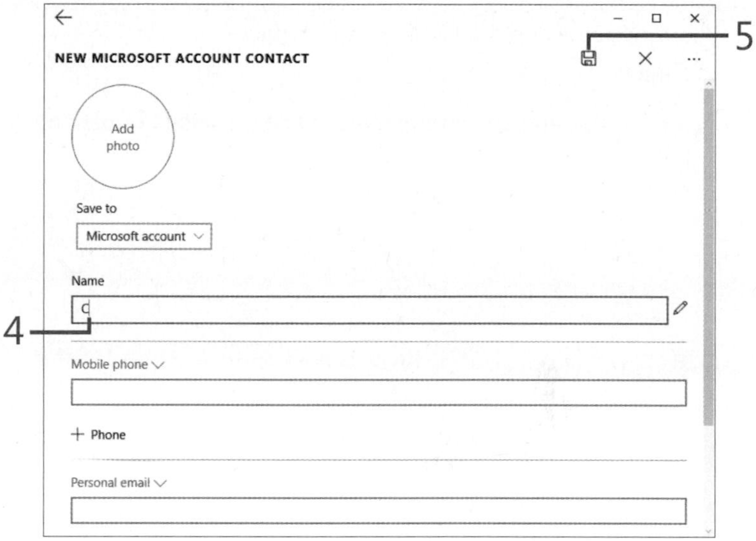

NEW MICROSOFT ACCOUNT CONTACT   ─5

Add photo

Save to

Microsoft account ∨

Name

4── C

Mobile phone ∨

+ Phone

Personal email ∨

→ **TRY THIS** You can link two contacts in the People app. When you do this, information for both contacts appear on each of their records. To find out more, see "Linking contacts" later in this section.

Editing contacts

Things change, and so do your contacts' phone numbers, email addresses, and even names. Editing the information for a contact is a simple matter of opening the contact's record, making any changes to the information it contains, and then saving the record.

Edit a contact

1 With the People app displayed, click a contact.

2 Click the Edit button.

3 Click a text box and add information or edit existing information.

4 Click Save.

> ✓ **TIP** If you change your mind, you can leave a contact form without saving edits by clicking the Close button to the right of the Save button.

Linking contacts

Linking contacts places all of the information for two or more contacts under one record. You might link a colleague and his assistant's contact information, for example, or link the records for your grandchildren so that you can find them in one spot.

Link contacts

1 With the People app open, click a contact.

2 Click the Link button.

3 Click the Choose A Contact To Link button.

4 Click a contact.

5 Click the Back button to return to the People home page.

TIP To edit a linked contact, select the contact you used to establish the link. Click the Edit button, and then click the linked contact's name. The record for that contact then opens for editing.

TIP To remove the link, on the home page, click the contact you used to establish the link, and then click the Link button. Click a contact listed there, and then click Remove.

Sharing contacts

People often want to share contact information for friends or coworkers. In the People app, you can share contact information easily. The methods that will be available to you might depend on what apps (such as Twitter or Mail) you have installed and set up.

Share a contact

1 With the People app open, in the left panel, click a contact.

2 In the right panel, click the See More button.

3 Click Share Contact.

4 Click an item to share, such as Mobile Phone or Home Address.

5 Click the Share button.

(continued on next page)

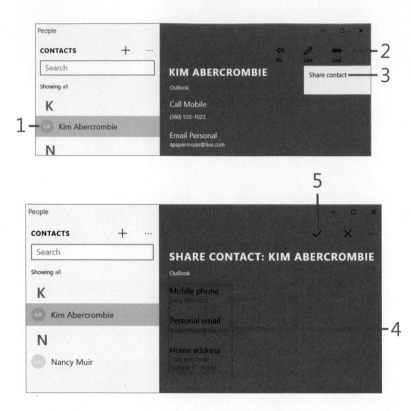

Share a contact *(continued)*

6 Click a Share option such as Mail.

7 In the form that opens, provide an addressee and any other information.

8 Click Send.

Using Mail

Email was one of the first forms of online communication, long before tweets and texting, and it's still very much in use today. In a business setting, email is still the go-to form of communication because it accommodates longer messages with larger attachments, and you can document those communications in a permanent way.

With the Mail app in Windows 10, you can set up email accounts you've created in services such as Outlook and Google Mail and access all your messages in one central location. Using the Mail app, you can receive, respond to, and forward email messages, and download email attachments. You can also use email folders to organize the messages you receive.

In this section:

- Setting up email accounts
- Reading email messages
- Opening an attachment
- Replying to a message
- Forwarding a message
- Creating a new message
- Formatting message text
- Adding attachments
- Moving emails to folders
- Deleting emails

Setting up email accounts

Before you can use an email account in Mail, you must set it up. The account actually exists in an email client such as Outlook or Yahoo!. By setting it up in Mail, you can access that account from the Mail app. You can set up multiple email accounts and switch among them easily. This makes it possible for you to have a central access point for your work email account and one or more personal accounts.

Set up an email account

1 Click the Start button.

2 Click the Mail tile.

3 If you've never used Mail before, you might need to click the Get Started button to proceed.

4 Click Add Account.

(continued on next page)

Set up an email account (continued)

5 Click the type of account that you want to set up.

6 Type your email address.

7 Type your password.

8 Click Sign In.

9 You might be asked to give permissions depending on the type of account you chose in step 5. When your account is set up, click the Done button.

TIP To add an account when you're signed in with another account, at the bottom of the left panel, click the Accounts button. (If the left panel isn't expanded click the Menu button in the top-left corner). Click the Add Account button that appears, and then continue with this procedure.

TRY THIS With more than one account created in Mail and one open, click the name of another account (located above the row of buttons at the bottom of the left panel). You switch to that account's inbox.

Choose an account

- Exchange
  Exchange, Office 365
- **5** — Outlook.com
  Outlook.com, Live.com, Hotmail, MSN
- Google
- iCloud

Add your Microsoft account

Sign in with your Microsoft account. You can use this account with other apps on this device. Learn more.

6 — someone@example.com

7 — Password

Forgot my password

No account? Create one!

Microsoft privacy statement

8 — Sign in   Cancel

Done — **9**

Reading email messages

Email is all about exchanging text messages and sometimes sharing attached documents. After you set up one or more mail accounts in Mail, when you click the Mail tile, you are taken to the Inbox of the last active account. From the Inbox, you can scroll to locate a message and then open and read it.

Open and read an email message

1 With an email account open in Mail, click a message to open and scroll through it.

2 Click the Back button to return to the Inbox.

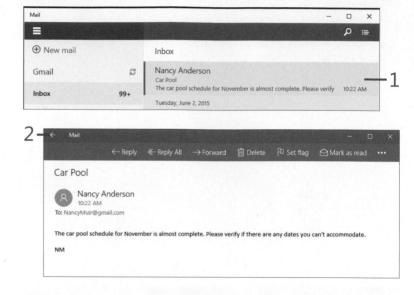

Opening an attachment

Some email messages that you receive contain an attachment. Attachments are files that are carried with the email that you can open and view or save. Attachments come in a variety of formats, based on the application in which they were saved.

Work with attachments

1 With the Mail app open and an Inbox selected, click a message with an attachment.

2 Click the attachment to open it.

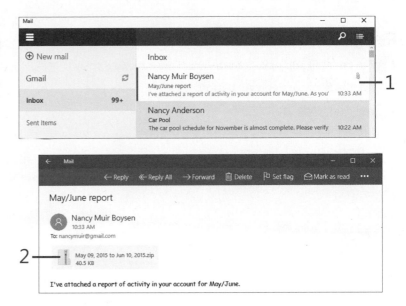

Replying to a message

When you read an email, you might want to reply to the sender or to the sender and all other recipients of the original message. When you open a message and choose a reply command, the message displays a new message area above the original contents. You then type your reply and send it.

Reply to email

1 With the Mail app open, click an email message to display it.

2 Click the Reply or Reply All button.

3 Type a message.

4 Click Send.

> **TIP** The choice between replying to just the sender or replying to the sender and all recipients is typically based on whether you want to share your response with all or only the original sender. For example, if you receive an email from someone organizing a meeting and you want to let him know you'll be five minutes late, does everybody else really need to receive and read your email?

Forwarding a message

Some messages are worth sharing. When you receive a message, in addition to replying to it, you have the ability to forward it to others. Any attachments to the original message will be forwarded, as well.

Forward a message

1 With the Mail app open and an email message displayed, click Forward.

2 In the To box, type one or more email addresses.

3 Type a message.

4 Click Send.

> ⚠️ **CAUTION** When you forward a message without the sender's permission, use your judgment about whether what you're sharing would be appropriate. If you think the sender has shared confidences or content with you that she would prefer remain private between you, forwarding the message or attachments might violate the sender's trust.

Creating a new message

Though you'll spend much of your time reading and replying to emails, you'll also spend time creating your own messages. You can send emails to a single recipient or a group of recipients. You can also copy people you consider tangential to the discussion but whom you want to keep informed. Finally, you can *blind carbon copy* those whom you want to keep in the loop but without other recipients being aware of them.

Create an email message

1 With the Mail app open, in the left panel, click the New Mail button.

2 Click the To box, and then type one or more addresses.

3 Click the Cc & Bcc link, if required, to open boxes in which you can add copy and blind-copy recipients addresses.

4 Click the Subject box, and then type a subject for the message.

5 Click Send.

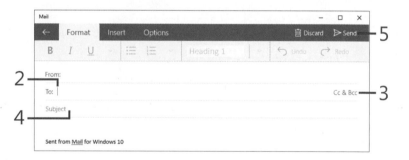

> **TIP** If you change your mind about sending the message, you can cancel it by clicking the Discard button, located near the top-right corner, to the left of the Send button.

> **TRY THIS** When creating a message, you can set its importance, language, and run a spelling check by clicking the Options button. Click the Importance, Language, and Spelling buttons to toggle between low and high importance, choose a language from a drop-down list, or run a spelling check before sending the message.

Formatting message text

You have probably used the tools in a word processing app to format text in documents, applying styles such as bold or italic, bullet or numbered lists, or setting font styles. Mail offers many of these same basic formatting tools, and you can use them to emphasize or organize text in your emails.

Format a message

1 With the Mail app open, click New Mail.

2 In the To box, type an email address.

3 Type a subject for the email.

4 Click in the message body, and then type a message.

5 Select the text, and then click the Bold, Italic, or Underline button.

6 Click the Styles drop-down list, and then select a style such as Emphasis.

7 Press Enter and type a second line of text.

8 Select both lines of text, and then click the Bullets button, selecting a style from the drop-down list that appears.

9 Click Discard to cancel the email or Send to send it.

> ✓ **TIP** You can click the arrow between the List and Styles options to display paragraph formatting. These options include indenting settings, text alignment and spacing settings, and spacing before and after paragraphs.

> ✓ **TIP** After you apply formatting, if you decide that you don't like the effect, use the Undo button to remove the formatting.

Adding attachments

Being able to attach documents of all kinds to emails gives you the ability you to communicate lengthier content quickly. Your attachments can be in any file format, though it might require that the recipient have the originating application on his computer to open it.

Attach a file

1 With a new email created in the Mail app, click the Insert tab.

2 Click Attach.

3 Browse to locate the file that you want to attach.

4 Click Open.

5 Click Send.

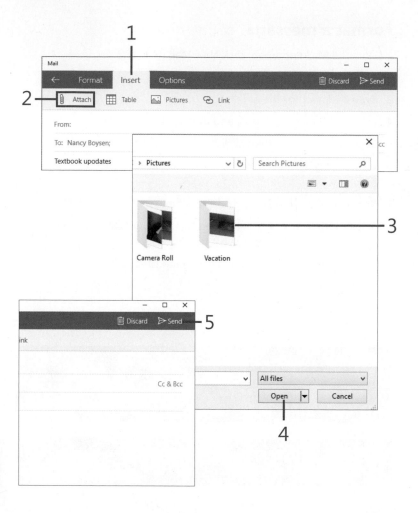

TIP If you save a document in PDF format, it can be opened by anybody who already has or downloads the free Adobe Reader app.

Moving emails to folders

You can organize the Inbox in your originating email account (such as Outlook or Gmail) into folders, and those folders will be available in the Mail app. In Mail, even though you can't create new folders, you can move emails that you receive in Mail into the existing folders from your email account. This helps you to keep a record of messages in an organized way.

Move email into a folder

1 With a message open in Mail, toward the top-right corner, click the Actions button.

2 Click Move.

3 Click a folder.

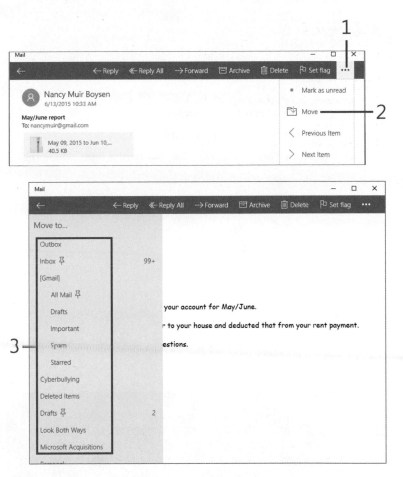

TIP To view all folders for an email account, at the bottom of the list of folders in the left panel of Mail, click the More button.

Deleting emails

You probably don't want to save every email message you get. Instead, you might prefer to delete certain messages after you read them. Deleted messages are actually saved in a Deleted Items folder for a time, but as that folder fills, older messages are purged from it. You can delete an open email by clicking the Delete button. To delete messages from your Inbox, you can use two methods.

Delete email

1 In the top-right corner of Mail, click the Select button.

2 Select a check box to the left of a message.

3 Click the Delete Selected Items button.

4 Move your mouse pointer over another message.

5 Click the Delete This Item button, located on the right side of the message itself.

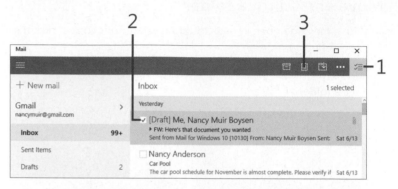

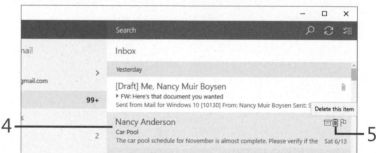

> **TIP** To delete multiple emails, use the Select button in Mail, and then select multiple check boxes before clicking the Delete Selected Items button. If you want to empty your Inbox or delete many messages at one time, it might be easier to go to the originating email service, use a Select All feature, and then delete the selected messages.

Shopping for apps in the Windows Store

The Windows Store is a handy way to download both free apps and those that you purchase, which you can then use on your Windows-based computer, tablet, or phone. The Store also includes music (see Section 13, "Enjoying music"), games (covered in Section 20, "Playing with Xbox games"), and movies and TV shows (see Section 14, "Recording and watching videos"). In this section, the focus is on buying apps. Apps provide you with functionality ranging from entertainment to maps to drawing. You can also get productivity applications such as Microsoft Word, PowerPoint, or Excel at the Windows Store.

Whether you buy an app in the Windows Store or choose one that is free, it is downloaded to your computer via an Internet connection. You can also download updated versions of apps you've purchased, either automatically or manually.

In this section:

- Exploring the Windows Store
- Creating payment information for an account
- Searching for apps
- Managing settings for updates
- Reading reviews
- Buying an app
- Rating an app

Exploring the Windows Store

The Apps section of the Windows Store includes a variety of collections and categories that help you to browse for apps. For example, across the top of the Store is a list of apps labeled Apps We Picked For You; this list is based on other purchases you've made. Beneath that, there are also lists of Top Free Apps as well as New And Rising Apps, Best Rated Apps, and so on as you scroll down the page.

Using the three links near the top of the page, you can explore by apps that are on top-rated charts, app categories (such as Business or Developer Tools), and collections of apps organized by topics such as Get Fit and Money and Budget.

You can also scroll to the bottom of the Apps home page and find even more categories such as Government & Politics, Kids & Family, and News & Weather.

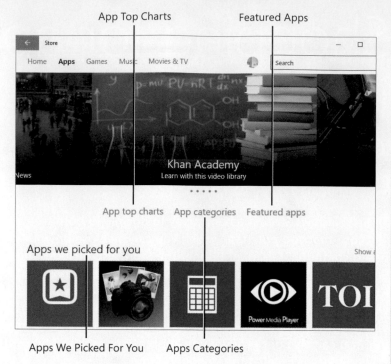

App Top Charts   Featured Apps

App top charts   App categories   Featured apps

Apps We Picked For You   Apps Categories

Categories

✓ **TIP** To see more apps in the lists that run across the Store screen, on the right side of the list, click the Show All link.

Searching for apps

You can use the built-in search feature in Windows Store to find apps either by providing the app name or a phrase about the type of app for which you're searching. A search will return results in several categories such as Albums, Songs, and TV Shows, as well as Apps.

Find an app

1 With the Windows Store open, click the Search box.

2 Type an app name or search term such as **calculator**.

3 Click the Search button.

4 Click an app to display details about it.

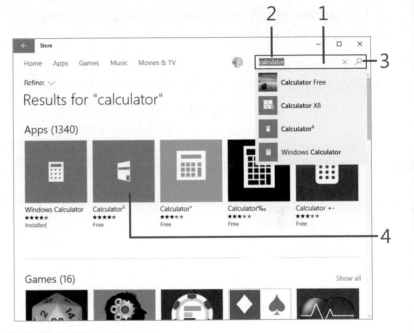

Creating payment information for an account

When you set up Windows 10 initially, you provided information about your Microsoft account or created a new account. To make purchases from the Windows Store, you need to add payment information to that account. After you have done that, you can make purchases using that account.

Add payment information to your account

1 Click the Start button.

2 Click the Store tile.

3 Click the Account button.

4 Click Payment Options and then sign in to your Microsoft account if requested.

(continued on next page)

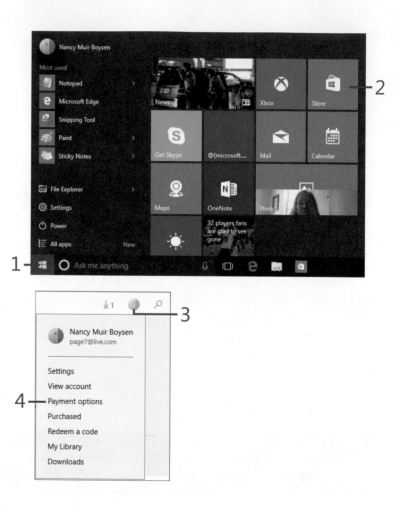

Add payment information to your account *(continued)*

5 Click the Payment & Billing tab.

6 Click Add Payment Option.

7 Add payment option details.

8 Click Next. Your new payment option details are confirmed.

TIP Each user account that you use to log in to Windows can have separate Payment & Billing settings. You can therefore pay for purchases from, say, your child's account using a different payment option than the one you use for your home business account.

Managing settings for updates

After you have purchased or downloaded a free app from the Windows Store, when an update to that app becomes available, you can download it from the Store. You can configure a setting so that updates to apps are applied automatically, or you can choose to initiate the updates yourself.

Make settings for updates

1 With the Windows Store open, click the Account button.

2 Click Settings.

3 Click the Update Apps Automatically switch to turn on or turn off automatic updating.

4 Click the Back button to return to the Store.

> ✓ **TIP** If you want to track updates that you have already down-loaded, you can click the Account button and then, in the menu that opens, select Downloads.

Reading reviews

Users of the Windows Store can rate the apps they obtain. Those ratings can help you and others make choices among apps. If you're not sure about whether to buy or download a free app, you should check out its reviews before you make your decision.

Read others' reviews

1 With the Windows Store open, click an app that you're considering buying.

2 Scroll down to the Ratings And Reviews section.

3 To be able to read all reviews, click Show All.

> **TIP** If you are reconsidering your purchase based on poor reviews, you might scroll down a bit further to see items listed in the People Also Like listing for similar products that might have received better reviews.

Buying an app

When you have set up payment options for your account, you can easily buy apps or content in the Windows Store. Some apps are free and some require that you purchase them; either way, obtaining and installing them works similarly.

Buy an app

1 In the Windows Store, locate an app that you'd like to own.

2 Click the app to open details about it.

3 Click the Price button.

4 Type your password.

5 Click Sign In.

6 Click Buy.

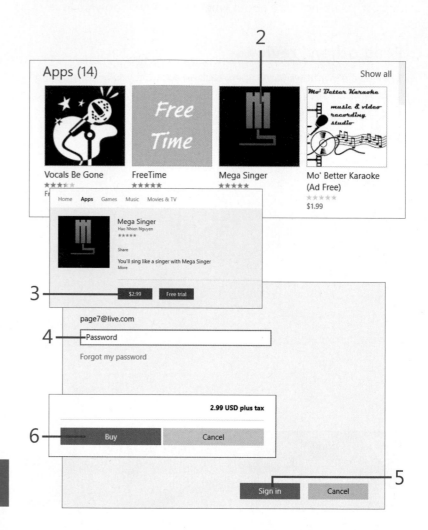

✓ **TIP** With many apps, you can try them out before buying. To do so, on the app details page, click the Free Trial button.

Rating an app

Just as reviews might have helped you find the right app for your need, your review of an app can help guide others. After you've used an app for a while, consider going back to the store to rate it.

Rate an app

1 With the details about an app displayed in the Windows Store, scroll down to the Ratings And Reviews section.

2 Click a star to rate the app from 1 to 5 (1 being the lowest rating, 5 the highest).

3 Type a headline.

4 Type a comment about what you like and don't like.

5 Click Submit.

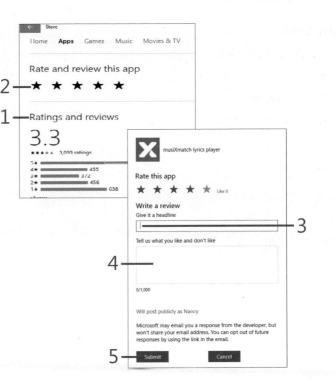

Enjoying music

13

For many people, listening to music on a computer has replaced using a fancy stereo system or radio. Computers make it possible for you to assemble a virtual music library taken from DVDs or downloaded from online sites. You can use your computer's speakers to deliver your music and use your computer controls to adjust volume and speaker settings.

The Music app in Windows 10 is your tool for buying music, playing music, and organizing music. In addition, the Cortana personal assistant built in to Windows 10 has a feature that helps you to identify music that's playing around you and to buy it.

In this section:

- Buying songs or albums
- Adding local music files
- Playing music
- Adjusting volume
- Searching for music
- Creating playlists
- Using Cortana to identify music

Buying songs or albums

You can buy music in the Windows Store and it will be available in the Music app. The Music app organizes music by song, album, or artist. You first must have created payment options for your Microsoft account to purchase music in the Windows Store. See "Creating payment information for an account" on page 150 for information about how to do this.

Buy and download music

1 Click the Start button.

2 Click the Groove Music tile.

If this is the first time you've opened music, click Go To Collection.

3 Click Get Music In Store.

(continued on next page)

Buy and download music *(continued)*

4 Click an album in any category such as New Albums, Top Albums, or a song under Top-Selling Songs.

5 Click the Price button to buy the album or to buy an individual track from the album.

6 Type your password.

7 Click Sign In.

8 Click Buy.

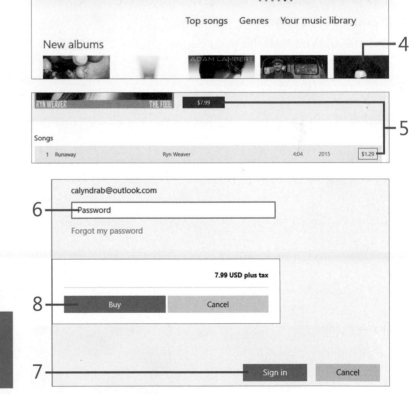

TIP Instead of choosing an item featured in the Music section of the Windows Store, you can search for an artist or album or even a musical genre such as jazz. See the task "Searching for music" later in this section.

Adding local music files

You don't have to get all your music from the Windows Store, You can add music to your computer that you've bought on your phone or have stored on another device or DVD, and then set up Music to check the folder where that music is stored. When it does, that music becomes available to you in the Music app.

Choose where Music checks for music files

1 With the Music app open, click the Settings button.

2 Click Choose Where We Look For Music On This PC.

3 Click the Add button.

4 Locate a folder; for example, Downloads.

5 Click the Add This Folder To Music button.

6 Click Done.

1 — ⚙

YOUR MUSIC

Music file location

Choose where we look for music on this PC — 2

Build your collection from your local music files
Right now, we're watching these folders:

3 — ⊕

| Downloads ×
C:\Users\Calyn\Downloads |

| Music ×
C:\Users\Calyn\OneDrive\Music | Music ×
C:\Users\Calyn\Calyn\Music |

Select Folder

← → ↑ ↓ › This PC › Downloads ∨ ↻

Organize ▾   New folder

Done — 6

- 📷 Pictures 📌
- 📄 Documents 📌
- ☁ OneDrive
- 💻 This PC
- 🖥 Desktop
- 📄 Documents
- 4 — ⬇ Downloads
- ♪ Music
- 📷 Pictures
- 📷 Videos
- 💽 OS (C:)

Name

No items match y

Folder: |

5 — Add this f

> **TIP** To view songs that are added to Music as a result of adding a local music file, on the left side of the Music app, click the Songs button.

Playing music

The main function of the Music app is to play music. After you've placed music in your Music app, playing it is simple. You first locate the piece of music or album that you want to play and then use the playback controls to play, pause, or move forward or backward one track at a time.

Play a song

1 With the Music app open, click the Songs button.

2 Click a song.

3 Click the Play button.

4 Click the Pause button to stop playback.

5 If you're playing an album, click the Back button to move to a different track. If you're playing an individual song, clicking this button brings you to the beginning of the song.

6 If you want the track to repeat when it ends, click the Repeat button.

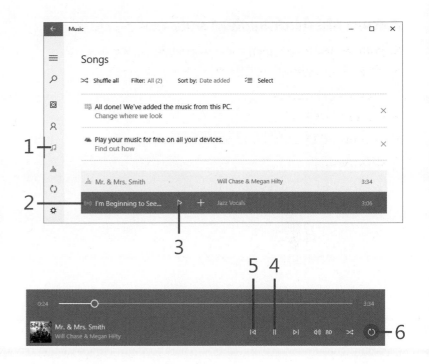

> ✓ **TIP** To play an entire album of music, in step 2, select an album rather than a song. To shuffle music in your library so that songs play in a random order, click the Shuffle button in the playback controls (it looks like two crossed arrows).

Adjusting volume

There are two volume settings that you can control: the system volume for your Windows 10 computer, and the playback volume in an app (such as the Music app). The system volume sets the overall level of volume for your device, and an app volume is set relative to that.

Adjust Music or system volume

1 With the Music app open and music playing, in the playback controls, click the Volume button.

2 Drag the volume slider to adjust the volume.

3 On the taskbar, click the Speakers/Headphones button.

4 Drag the volume slider to adjust volume.

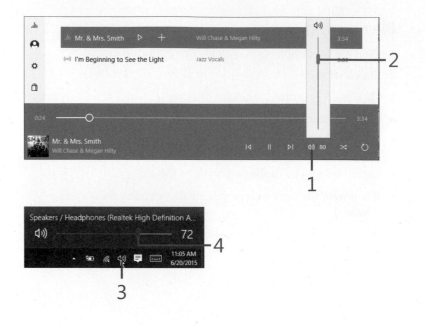

 TIP To fine tune your speaker and system sound volume, right-click the Speakers/Headphones button, and then, from the shortcut menu that opens, choose Open Volume Mixer. You can then adjust the speaker volume and system sound volume (for example, for notifications of new emails) separately.

Searching for music

After you assemble a large library of music, you might need to locate the song or album that you want to play. You can use the Search feature in the Music app to find what you need by typing search terms for a song title, album name, genre, or artist.

Find music

1 With the Music app open, click the Search field and type a search term.

2 Click to choose a suggestion or press Enter to view results.

Creating playlists

The ability to create a playlist makes it possible for you to assemble your own virtual albums from more than one source. You might create one playlist of dance music, another for your next party, and still another for a romantic evening at home. You can create as many playlists as you like from the music you have available in the Music app.

Create a new playlist

1 With the Music app open, click New Playlist.

2 Type a name for the playlist.

3 Click Save.

4 Click the list.

5 Click Add Songs.

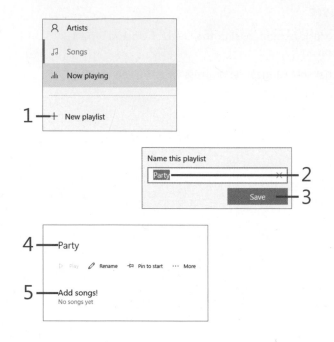

> **✓ TIP** To place a playlist on the Start menu so that you can quickly play it, from the playlist screen, click Pin To Start. To unpin it, go back to the playlist screen and click Unpin From Start.

Using Cortana to identify music

Do you like that tune playing on the radio, in the elevator, or in a café? Cortana, the new personal assistant In Windows 10, has the ability to identify music that's currently playing. After

Cortana identifies music, you can follow a link to Xbox Music to find out more about the song or purchase it.

Identify music that's playing

1 With a song playing, say, "Hey Cortana," or in the Cortana search box, click the microphone button.

2 Say, "What's this song?"

3 When Cortana identifies the music, you can click it to go to the song (or an album) in the Windows Store to buy it.

> ⊘ **TIP** Cortana's ability to identify music is pretty sophisticated. She is capable of searching thousands of songs; however, she won't help you find more obscure music, nor can Cortana identify a song you sing to her. Cortana bases the results on recordings in her database.

Recording and watching videos

Today, computers are used as much to play video as they are to create word processed reports. With Windows 10, you can use the Camera app to capture your own videos, the Movies & TV app to buy programs and play them back, and the old workhorse, Windows Media Player, to organize media into playlists and play media.

In this section, you make use of all three apps to create or locate content and use playback controls to watch videos. You also use the Windows Store to buy or rent video content and open up a world of available programs.

In this section:

- Recording your own videos by using the Camera app
- Buying videos
- Locating videos in the Movies & TV app
- Playing videos
- Configuring settings in the Movies & TV app
- Playing video by using Windows Media Player
- Creating playlists by using Windows Media Player

Recording your own videos by using the Camera app

Most computers are equipped with a camera with which you can capture still photos or create video recordings. With Windows 10, you use the Camera app to record video and then view the recorded video in the Photos app. You can also playback your personal videos by using the Movies & TV app.

Record a video

1 Click the Start button.

2 In the All Apps list, click the Camera app.

3 Click the Video button once to switch to video mode.

4 Click the Video button again to begin recording.

5 Click the Video button again to stop recording.

6 Click the Photos button to open the Photos app and play the video.

 TIP To playback a video you've recorded, open the Photos app and choose Collection. Click the Play button on the video that you want to watch.

Buying videos

The Windows Store offers a wide variety of movies and TV shows that you can rent or buy. First, you must have set up payment options for your Microsoft account (for instructions on how to do this, see the task "Creating payment information for an account" on page 150). After you're set up, you can use the Shop feature in the Movies & TV app to go directly to that category and make purchases. When you purchase TV shows, you have the option of buying a season pass or individual episodes.

Shop for movies

1 Open the Movies & TV app.

2 Click the Shop For Movies & TV button.

3 Click a movie.

4 Click the Buy button.

5 Type your password.

6 Click Sign In.

7 Click Buy to purchase the movie.

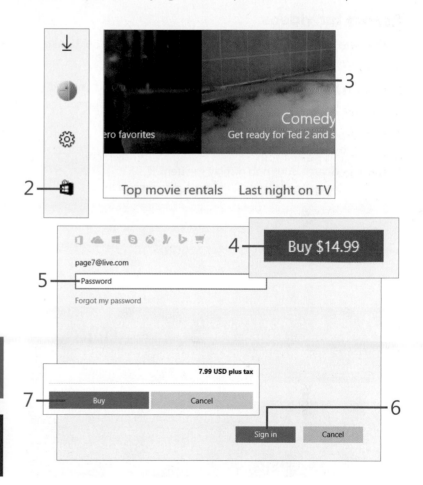

> **TIP** In step 4, you can also click the Rent button. If you do, you'll be asked if you want to stream or download the movie before proceeding with signing in to your account.

> **TRY THIS** When you open the detail window for a movie, you will quite often find a button for watching a trailer. Click this to view the trailer for the movie before making your buying decision.

Locating videos in the Movies & TV app

After you have purchased a number of videos, there are a few tools that you can use to locate those videos. The app divides videos by movies, TV shows, and personal videos. You can also use the Search tool to locate videos by name, no matter what category in which they are saved.

Search for videos

1 With the Movies & TV app open, click the Movies button if you're searching for a movie.

2 If you're looking for a TV show, click the TV button.

3 If you're looking for a personal video, click the Videos button.

4 Click the Search button.

5 Type the title for a movie, video, or TV show.

6 Click the Search button to display the item.

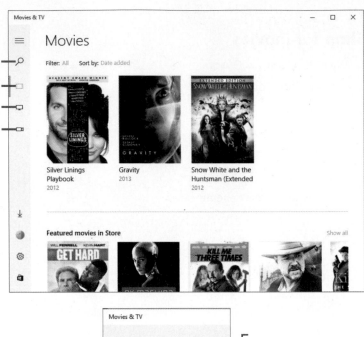

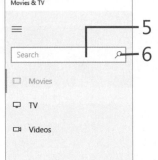

> **✓ TIP** Personal videos that you record with the Camera app are assigned names such as 0604150534. You might want to locate the file in File Explorer, right-click it, and rename it so that it's easier to search for in future.

> **✓ TIP** You can use the Filter and Sort By fields at the top of the Movies and TV windows to organize videos. With Filter, you can sort by videos on your computer or in the cloud. Sort By lets you sort by the date the video was added to your library or alphabetically.

Playing videos

When you have recorded, downloaded, or rented a video, you can play it in the Movies & TV app. You can use the playback controls to pause, adjust the aspect ratio, adjust volume, turn on closed captioning for shows that support that feature, and expand the video image.

Play a video

1 With the Movies & TV app open, click a video title.

2 Click the Play button.

3 Click the Full-Screen button.

4 Click the playback slider to move to a later moment in the video.

5 Click the Pause button.

 TIP You can use a playback tool named Cast To Device to cast the movie to a compatible device such as a smart TV. To cast a video to a smart TV, it must be on and have a Bluetooth connection.

 TIP The Aspect Ratio button changes the view from a shadow-box display to a display with no surrounding shadow box.

Configuring settings in the Movies & TV app

You can play video at different quality settings, which can have an impact on your viewing experience. Within the Movies & TV app are settings that help you to control the quality of video playback and where the app looks for videos on your computer.

Configure settings for video quality and downloads

1 With the Movies & TV app open, click the Settings button.

2 Click either the HD or SD option to choose that quality setting as the default.

3 Click the Choose Where We Look For Videos link.

(continued on next page)

Configure settings for video quality and downloads *(continued)*

4 Click the Add button.

5 Locate a folder that you want to add.

6 Click Add This Folder To Videos.

7 Click Done.

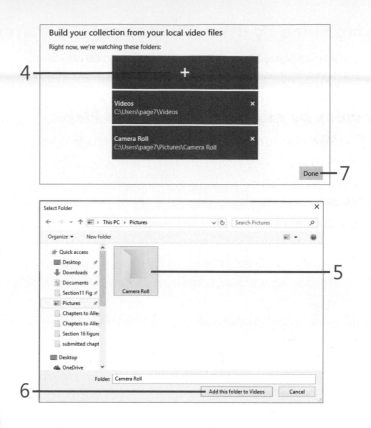

> ✓ **TIP** If you have more than one Windows device—for example, a PC, a Surface tablet, and a Windows Phone—you can access downloaded videos and rentals from them all. Use the Show My Download Devices link in the Settings window of the app to view available devices.

> ✓ **TIP** To make changes to your account billing or other information, use the links under the heading More, on the right side of the Settings window.

Playing video by using Windows Media Player

Windows Media Player has been around for many iterations of Windows. This player is an option to the Movies & TV or Music apps with which you can play music as well as personal videos, and display pictures.

Play video by using Windows Media Player

1 Click the Start button, and then, in the All Apps list, click Windows Media Player.

2 Click the Videos folder.

3 Double-click a video to play it.

4 Use the playback controls to control playback.

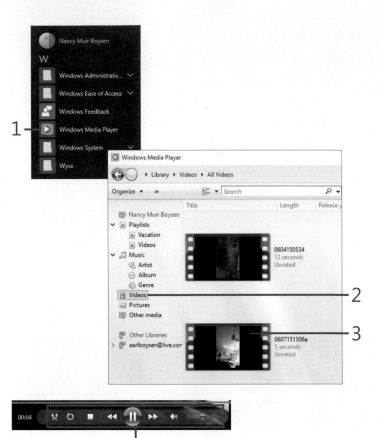

> ✓ **TIP** The playback controls in Windows Media Player don't offer features such as closed captioning and casting a video to a smart TV, which are available in the Movies & TV app.

Creating playlists by using Windows Media Player

You can also create playlists of music or video. For example, if you want to assemble three videos from your child's birthday party into one playlist to play them one after the other, you can do so in Windows Media Player.

Create a playlist

1   With Windows Media Player open to full screen, click Create Playlist.

2   Type a name for the new playlist.

3   Click the Videos folder to display videos.

4   In the Navigation pane, drag videos to the playlist.

5   To play the playlist, in the left pane, double-click it.

✓ **TIP**   To remove a video from a playlist open the playlist, and then right-click the video. On the shortcut menu that opens, click Remove From List.

Working with the Camera and Photos apps

Though you might be used to taking photos with your smartphone, you might be unaware that your computer probably has a built-in camera. Using the Camera app that comes with Windows 10, you can take pictures of your surroundings. You can then use the Photos app to edit those photos in a variety of ways. Photos offers tools that you can use to enhance a photo, apply effects, adjust brightness, and crop or rotate it.

You can also create a slideshow from your photos and share them with others. Of course, if you no longer need a photo, you can easily delete it.

In this section:

Taking photos or videos by using the Camera app

In a computer, the camera is typically placed above the monitor, whether you own a laptop or desktop model. When you turn on the Camera app, the camera takes pictures of whoever or whatever is facing the monitor. The main purpose of a computer camera is to capture video of the person using the computer for an online video call.

Snap a photo

1 Click the Start button.

2 Click All Apps

3 Scroll down, and then click Camera.

4 Position your computer so that it's aimed at what you want to capture, and then click the Capture button.

5 Click the Photos button to open Photos with the photo displayed.

> **TIP** Photos that you take with the Camera app are saved to the Camera Roll folder within the Picture folder. The Photos app organizes photos into collections, such as those taken on a certain day, and albums that are created for you containing the best in a series of shots taken around the same time.

Editing photos by using the Photos app

We're not all professional photographers, and, unsurprisingly, our photos aren't always perfect. So, it's useful that you can edit a photo after you take it. The Photos app provides several useful tools for editing photos. For example, you can apply filters that change the hue of the picture, or you can modify the light to brighten an image or apply higher contrast.

Use photo editing tools

1 In the Start menu, click the Photos tile to open the app, and then click a photo in a Collection to display it.

2 Click the Edit button.

3 Click the Filters button.

4 On the right side of the screen, select a filter to apply it.

5 Click the Light button.

6 On the right, click either Brightness or Contrast.

7 Drag the button up or down to move the setting indicator (the white arc) around the button, and observe the changes.

> (→) **TRY THIS** Continue to explore the other editing tools such as Color and Effects to see what options they have to offer. Their settings work in the same way as those for the Light settings.

Enhancing a photo

If you don't want to play around with applying different settings such as light and filters, you can use a single enhancement tool that applies multiple setting changes to produce what the Photos app "considers" to be the best photo possible.

Enhance an image

1 With the Photos app open and the Edit tools displayed, click Basic Fixes if it's not already selected.

2 Click Enhance.

3 If you're not satisfied with the result, click the Undo button to cancel the enhancements.

4 When you're satisfied, click the Save button.

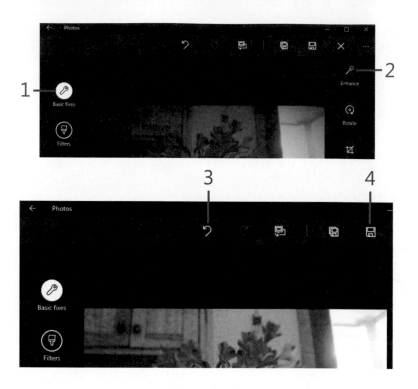

 TRY THIS Experiment with the Selective Focus tool which is available when you click the Effects button in the editing screen. With this tool, you can pinpoint the area on the photo that should have the crispest focus. You also can selectively enhance that area.

Cropping photos

Just as not every photo we take comes out as bright as we'd like, some include items we never intended to include. By cropping your photo, you can whittle away sections that you don't want, leaving just the portions of the image that you want to keep.

Crop photos in the Photos app

1 With the Photo app open and the Edit tools displayed, click Basic Fixes if it's not already selected.

2 Click the Crop button.

3 Drag any corner handle inward.

4 When the image appears as you want, release your mouse button.

5 Click the Apply button (the check mark) to confirm the changes.

> ✓ **TIP** You can drag the handles on an image to be cropped inward, outward, to the right, left, up, or down.

> ✓ **TIP** While using the Crop tool, you can click the Aspect Ratio button at the top of the screen to set parameters for the changes in your image's size. You can, for example, indicate you want the cropped image to be square, maintain the original aspect ratio, or display as widescreen.

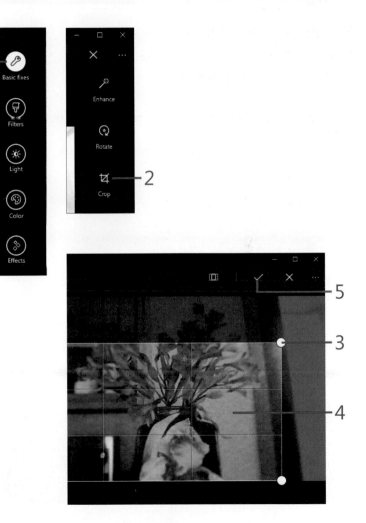

Cropping photos: Crop photos in the Photos app **181**

Rotating photos

Though you're not likely to hold your computer upside down and therefore capture an image upside down, you might want to rotate a photo to place it in a document at an angle as a special effect. The Photos app offers a Rotate tool with which you can pivot an image in 90-degree increments.

Rotate a photo

1 With the editing tools displayed in the Photos app and Basic Fixes selected, click the Rotate button.

2 Click the Rotate button again to continue rotating the image clockwise.

3 If you want to undo a rotation, click the Undo button.

✓ **TIP**   Rather than clicking the Undo button, another way to revert the image to its original orientation is to simply click the Rotate button until it's back to where it started.

Viewing albums

If you choose Collection on the Photos home page, you see every image you've taken organized by the month in which they were taken. The Photos app also creates an album named Camera Roll to organize photos for you. By default, this album contains all of the photos you take with the Camera app, grouped by date taken. In addition, new albums are created for you over time. For example, if you take a series of pictures around the same time, Photos will create an album containing the best of those images.

Look at albums in Photos

1 With the Photos app open, click Collection.

2 Scroll down to view all of the photos you've taken, organized by month taken.

3 Click Albums.

4 Click an album to open it and display its contents.

TIP As of this writing, Photos doesn't allow you to create your own albums or rename the albums the Photos app creates for you.

Working with photos in Paint

The Photos app offers many tools for editing photos. Still, the Paint app, which is part of Windows Accessories, can take you even further. The Paint app offers tools for drawing with a Pencil or Brush tool to circle or point to items in a photo as well as the ability to draw a text box on a photo and enter descriptive text or quotes about the image.

Edit photos in Paint

1 On the Start menu, in the All Apps list, click Paint to open the app (it's in the Windows Accessories section).

2 Click File.

3 Click Open.

4 Locate and click an image, and then click the Open button.

(continued on next page)

Edit photos in Paint *(continued)*

5 Click the Resize button to display resizing options.

6 Click the Rotate button to display rotation options.

7 Click the Pencil button, and then draw or write on the image.

8 Click the Eraser tool to erase anything you've drawn.

9 Click the Text button to draw a box on the image, and then type any text you want in it.

10 In the palette on the right, click a color.

11 Click the Brushes button, and then choose a brush style.

12 Use your mouse to brush color onto the image.

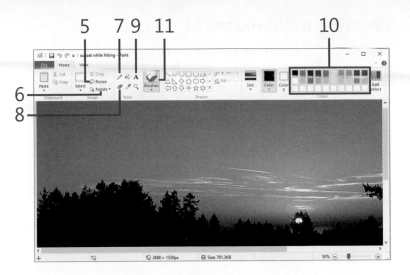

TIP There are other editing tools in Paint with which you can make your text boxes opaque or transparent, modify the font used in text boxes, and so on. Explore Paint to discover how many editing tools it offers.

Creating a slideshow

One photo can show a moment in time, but several photos shown sequentially can tell a story. Using the Photos app, you can create a slideshow from a collection of photos. With the slideshow feature, you can display one photo after another and stop the slideshow at any time.

Create and run a slideshow

1 With the Photos app open to the home screen, click a photo in a collection to open it.

2 Click the Slideshow button to begin the slideshow.

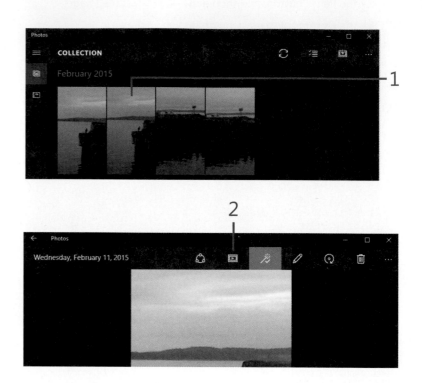

Setting a photo as your lock screen or desktop background

If you have a favorite photo, rather than frame it and put it on your desk, why not make it the image for your desktop or lock screen background? With a photo displayed in the Photos app you can set it up to be used as the background to either your desktop or the lock screen that appears when your computer has gone to sleep.

Set photo as a background

1 With a photo displayed in the Photos app, click the More button.

2 Click Set As Lock Screen or Set As Background.

3 Click the Close button.

TIP To stop using the photo as a background, right-click the desktop, and then, in the shortcut menu that opens, choose Personalization, and then choose a different background from Windows pictures, or a solid color.

Sharing photos

When you take a great photo it's hard to avoid the urge to share it with others. With the Photos app, you can share photos via Facebook, Twitter, or the Mail app. After you set up the Mail app to use one or more email accounts, it's a simple procedure to send a photo by email. (See Section 11, "Using Mail," for more about how to do this.)

Share a photo via email

1 With a photo displayed in the Photos app, click the Share button.

2 Click Mail.

3 If you have more than one email account, click to select the account that you want to use.

4 Type an email address.

5 Type a subject.

6 Type a message.

7 Click Send.

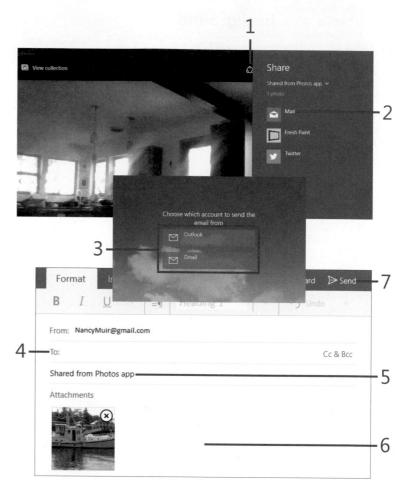

TRY THIS To share via Facebook or Twitter, you need to have those apps already installed and have accounts set up.

TIP If you want to share a hard copy of a photo, display it in the Photos app, and then click the More button. Click Print, and then use the dialog box that appears to print your photo.

Deleting photos

If your Photo collections become crowded over time, making it difficult to find what you need, you might consider deleting some photos. You can delete a single photo or select several to delete in one action.

Delete photos

1 With a photo collection displayed on the Photos home screen, select the check box for one or more photos to choose them.

2 Click the Delete button.

3 In the confirmation prompt that appears, click Delete.

⚠️ **CAUTION**   Deleting a photo in the Photos app also deletes it in the Photos folder in File Explorer.

Keeping on schedule with Calendar

Using the Calendar app included with Windows 10, you can view calendars, create events, and share those events with others via email. You can view calendars by day, week, or month. You can even view your work week only, leaving weekends out of the picture.

You can include special calendars such as a Birthday calendar or US Holidays calendar in your display, so that all events on these calendars appear in line with your own calendar events. The Birthday calendar will include birthdays of your Facebook friends.

In this section:

- Displaying Calendar
- Changing views
- Adding an event
- Using Cortana to add an event
- Inviting people to an event
- Editing an event
- Changing work week settings
- Displaying US Holidays and Birthday calendars
- Deleting an event

Displaying Calendar

The Calendar app displays as a tile on the Start menu by default. When you open it, the current month appears in the top-left pane. You also see a pane that you can adjust to show a larger calendar by day, week, work week, or month. You can switch among months, both past and future, as well.

Open the Calendar app

1 Click the Start button.

2 Click the Calendar tile.

3 Click the Forward or Back button to view the next or previous month.

> ✓ **TIP** The controlling calendar will be displayed under the left calendar pane. By default, this will be the Outlook calendar with your name+Calendar, Birthday Calendar, and US Holidays calendar selected.

Changing views

With your Calendar programs, you can view your schedule by the day, week, or month. In addition, the Calendar app built in to Windows 10 gives you the ability to view your work week, whether that week runs from Sunday through Thursday or Monday through Friday.

View different time increments

1 With the Calendar app open, on the Day tab, click the drop-down arrow.

2 On the drop-down menu, click 3 Day.

3 Click the Week button.

4 Click the Month button.

5 Click the Work Week button.

TIP If you have moved to a display that doesn't show the current date, in the top-right corner, click the Today button to shift timeframes to include today's date.

Adding an event

The entire point of a calendar app is to give you the means to schedule various events, from a luncheon to a business meeting, and have the app remind you of an upcoming occasion.

With the Calendar app, you can create an event and specify the time and length for that event as well as a location. You can even choose which calendar to display it on, such as My Calendar or the Birthday calendar.

Create a new event

1 With the Calendar app open, click a date.

2 Type an Event Name.

3 In the Start Time and End Time boxes, click the drop-down arrows, and then set a time for each.

4 Click the Location box, and then type a location.

5 Click Done.

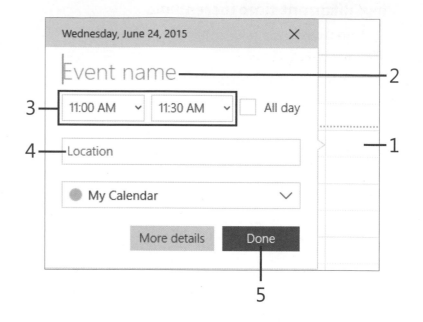

TIP To indicate that an event will last the entire day, select the All Day check box, located to the right of the Start Time and End Time boxes.

Using Cortana to add an event

Cortana is your personal assistant, and as such, she can search the Internet, open apps, identify music, and even set an appointment for you.

By speaking your appointment details to Cortana rather than typing them, you have a hands-free way to add events to your calendar.

Ask Cortana to create an event

1 Click the Cortana search box.

2 Click the microphone button.

3 Ask Cortana to add an event to your calendar.

4 Click the subject, date, and time fields and speak or type specifics about the appointment.

Inviting people to an event

When you create an event such as a meeting or party, you can use the Calendar app to include other people in the event. By inviting others, you notify them of the event details and give

them a way to convey their intentions by replying Yes, No, or Maybe.

Invite others to an event

1 With the Calendar app open, click a date to add an event.

2 Enter event details such as name, start, and finish times.

3 Click More Details.

4 Click the Invite Someone box.

5 Type an email address, and then press Enter.

6 Click Send.

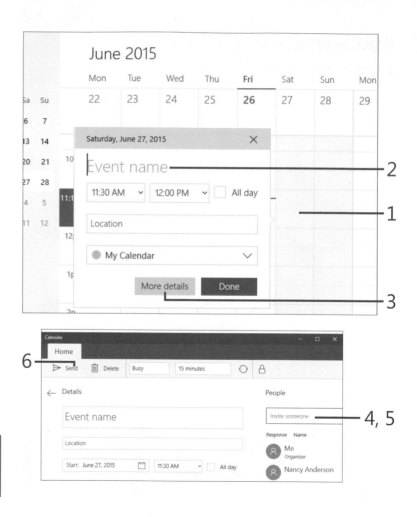

> ✓ **TIP** When those who receive an invitation respond—whether to accept or refuse the invitation—you'll receive emails from these people in your default email account.

Editing an event

Sometimes, your plans change. When you want to edit an event to change the date, time, or invitees, you can do so easily and even inform everyone of the changes at the same time.

Note that being able to simply change the date saves you the effort of deleting a task on one day and adding it on another.

Edit event details

1 With the Calendar app open, click an event to which you've invited people.

2 Make changes to any field.

3 Right-click the name of an invitee.

4 Click Remove.

5 Click Send Update.

> **TIP** If you have invited people to the event and you make changes to it, click the Send Update button in step 5 to save changes and inform invitees of the change.

Changing work week settings

If you use your computer for work-related activities, you might want to designate the days that comprise your work week. For example, if you work Monday through Friday and click the Work

Week view, you will no longer see Saturday or Sunday displayed. If you choose Thursday through Sunday, you have a four-day work week. You can also set working hours.

Choose your work week

1 With the Calendar app open, click the Settings button.

2 Click Calendar Settings.

3 Click the First Day Of Week box, and then choose the starting day of your week.

4 Click the end day of the week, either 5 or 6 days after the start of the work week.

5 Click the Start Time and End Time boxes and choose relevant times.

6 Click back in the Calendar to close the Calendar Settings pane and save your changes.

> ✓ **TIP**   Changes to your work week only affect the Work Week view. The Week and Month views will still show the entire calendar.

Displaying the US Holidays and Birthday calendars

Your email account might contain certain secondary calendars whose contents you can display on your calendar. For example, Outlook calendars can include United States holidays and birthdays. And, birthdays can be placed on your calendar by social networking sites such as Facebook.

Display special calendars

1 With the Calendar app open, click your Calendar to remove all of the events that you've entered using this email account.

2 Click US Holidays to remove notations of holidays.

3 Click Birthday Calendar to remove automatic friends' birthdays from a social-networking site such as Facebook.

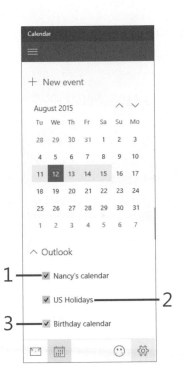

✓ **TIP** To reinstate any of these calendars on your Calendar app, just click it again. When a calendar check box is filled with a color (rather than white), it's displayed.

Deleting an event

Our schedules change, in spite of our best efforts to organize ourselves. Sometimes, it can be something as simple as an appointment being cancelled. Deleting an event from the Calendar app is simple and helps you to avoid getting a notification about an event that's no longer going to happen.

Remove an event from your calendar

1   Click an event to open its Details page.

2   Click Delete.

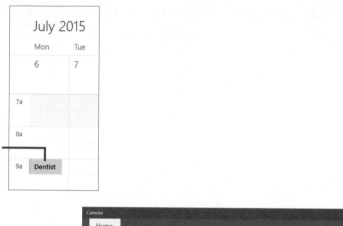

 TIP   You can't delete individual events on the US Holidays or Birthday calendars.

Tracking your sports, news, stocks, and fitness

Windows 10 includes several preinstalled apps such as Sports, News, Money, and Health & Fitness. Each app boasts some pretty robust features, so the purpose of this section is to introduce you to some of the more interesting ones. Feel free to explore each app on your own to discover even more functionality.

In this section:

- Reading news articles
- Adding and turning off interests
- Choosing a sports category
- Adding a Sports favorite
- Creating an investment Watchlist
- Viewing markets
- Using Diet Tracker
- Creating a profile

Reading news articles

You can use the News app included with Windows 10 to keep you up to speed on current new stories. You can view the news articles in various categories such as US, World, Crime, and Technology. You can also permit MSN News to access your location so that you can receive local news.

Read the news

1 Click the Start button.

2 Click the News tile.

3 At the top of the screen, click a category of news.

4 Click a news story to read it.

5 Drag the scrollbar to read more of the article.

6 Click the Forward button to view another story.

> ✓ **TIP** If your interests tend toward video news, click the Menu button, and then click Videos. The News app will display videos related to current news items. You can also use the Search box in the News app to search for stories related to a word or phrase.

Adding and turning off interests

Not everyone shares the same interests, so the News app gives you the option to pick and choose what topics to include in your news. For example, you might leave out World news and include only US news, or add interests such as animals or religion.

Add or turn off a topic of interest

1 With the News app open, click the Interests button.

2 Click the green check mark for a topic to turn it off.

3 Click the Add An Interest button.

4 In the Search box, type a term. In the suggested results, click an item to select it or click the Search button for more results.

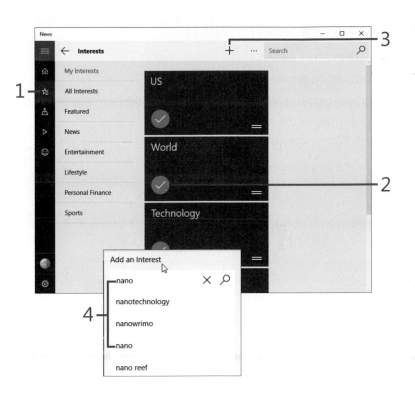

TIP If you have a category of interest that doesn't fit within the broad category of interests that the News app provides, use the Search box to type a term related to that interest, such as "Broadway," and then click the Search button to view matches.

Choosing a sports category

Most sports addicts have their favorite games, teams, and athletes. Some might like football, baseball, and basketball, but how many also like hockey, golf, soccer, and tennis? If this description fits you, you'll enjoy the Sports app and how you can choose the sports news that you want to review.

Display a sports category

1 Click the Start button.

2 Click the Sports tile.

3 On the left side, click a button to display articles within a sports category such as Golf or Major League Soccer.

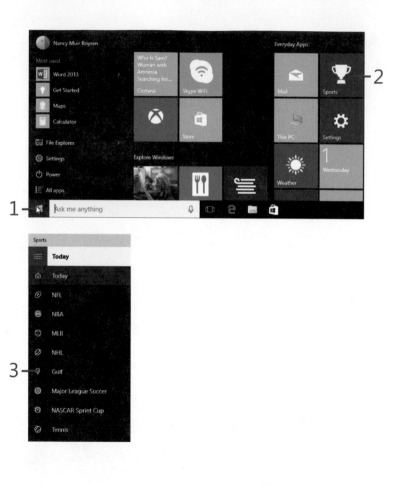

TIP There are quite a few sports categories. To make a particular category easier to find, in the top-left corner, click the Menu button to add titles to the icons.

Adding a sports favorite

Just as you can customize many apps to display your favorite activities or categories, you can customize the Sports app to add favorites. Using the Favorites feature, you can follow a particular sport or team, saving you time as you peruse all the sports and scores that are out there.

Add a favorite sport or team

1 With the Sports app open, click the My Favorites button.

2 Click the Add button.

3 Type a team name.

4 Click a team name in the search results.

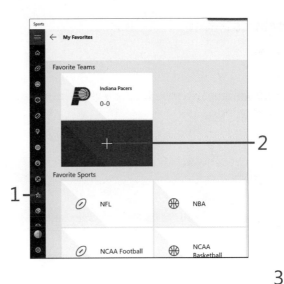

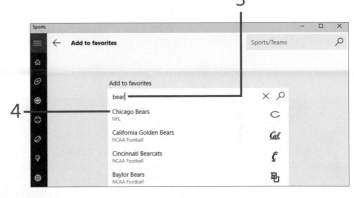

> **✓ TIP** To view the latest scores when you're on the Sports home screen, near the top-left corner, click the Scoreboard tab. This displays a tile for each game currently underway. Click one to display up-to-date results.

Adding a sports favorite: Add a favorite sport or team **205**

Creating an investment Watchlist

One of the great features of the Money app in Windows 10 is the ability to create a Watchlist that includes the investments that interest you most. This list can include stocks and other investments, and you can use it to easily track the latest valuations for your investments.

Create a Watchlist

1 Click the Start button.

2 Click the Money tile.

3 Click Watchlist.

4 Click the Add To Watchlist button.

5 Type a company name or stock exchange abbreviation.

6 Click a result to add it to your Watchlist.

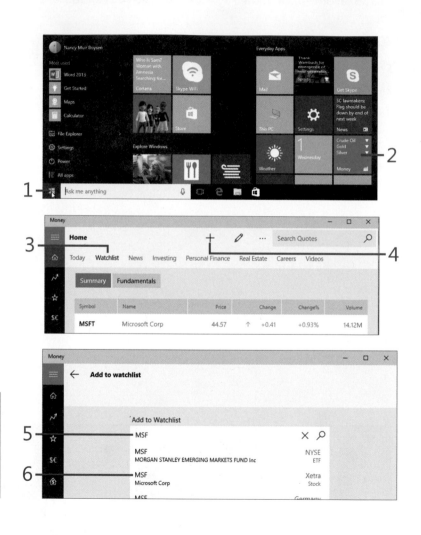

> ✅ **TIP** If keeping track of global currencies is important to your investment scheme, with the Money app open, on the left side of the screen, in the Navigation list, click the Currencies button. Here, you can locate current values for major world currencies and view trends for currency valuations and exchange rates, such as USD to EURO.

Viewing markets

The Money app can provide information about markets in the Unites States, which include stocks, commodities, bonds, and more. This information, which includes trends and up-to-the-minute rates for loans and credit cards, can be very useful when plotting your investment strategies.

View stock markets

1 With the Money app open, click the Markets button.

2 Click a tab such as Movers to display related exchanges.

3 Click a stock exchange to reveal a detailed chart and statistics.

4 Click the scrollbar to review a detailed chart and statistics.

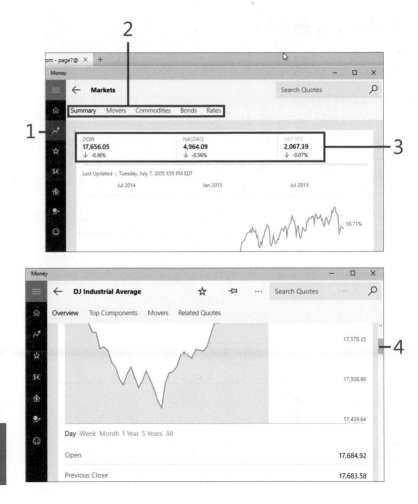

TIP Continue to scroll down the page for a market such as the Dow Jones to read recent news stories relevant to that exchange from various financial publications.

Using Diet Tracker

Using the Health & Fitness app that comes with Windows 10, you can read the latest articles about nutrition, exercise, and diet. You can also track your personal exercise and diet, check symptoms of medical conditions, and investigate medications. This section introduces you to one of the popular features of this app: Diet Tracker.

Track your diet

1 Click the Start button.

2 Click the Health & Fitness tile.

3 Click Diet Tracker.

4 Click the Add Food button for a meal such as Lunch.

(continued on next page)

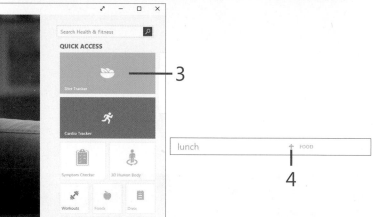

Track your diet *(continued)*

5 Click a recent or favorite food or, in the Search box, type a food.

6 Click the food to add it to your day's diet.

7 Click Done.

Add Food

recent · favorite · custom · Search

+ Italian Bread	★	1	1 slice, medium	54 Cal
+ Navel Oranges	★	1	1 fruit (2-7/8" dia)	69 Cal
+ Pad Thai Noodles - A Taste...	★	1	1 cup prepared	240 Cal
+ Pinot Blanc Wine	★	3	1 5 fl oz serving	363 Cal
+ Sliced Turkey Breast - Harve...	★	1	2 slices	60 Cal
+ Roasted, Salted & Shelled Pi...	★	1	1/4 cup	160 Cal
+ Raspberries	★	1	1 cup	64 Cal

TODAY LUNCH

DONE

✓ **TIP** Check out the Food & Drink app to get more information about nutrition, add recipes, and create shopping lists and meal plans.

Creating a profile

To use the features of the Health & Fitness app most effectively, you can personalize your profile. With the My Profile feature, you can specify your gender, age, height, and weight. You can also set a Calorie Target and even specify the types of exercise that you prefer.

Customize your profile

1 With the Health & Fitness app open, click My Profile.

2 Click in various fields, and then choose or provide information about you.

3 To view daily caloric intake recommendations, click My Calorie Target.

4 Click My Fitness Preferences.

(continued on next page)

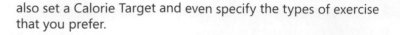

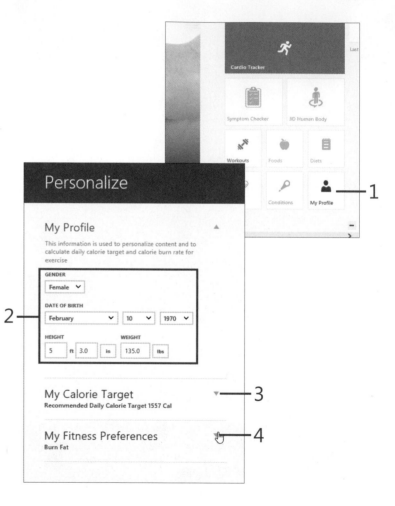

Customize your profile *(continued)*

5 To add any activities that you are interested in, click the associated Add button.

6 In the I Want To category, click your goals.

Personalize

My Profile ▼
Female, 45 yrs, 135.0 lbs, 5'3.0"

My Calorie Target ▼
Recommended Daily Calorie Target 1557 Cal

My Fitness Preferences ▲
Personalize featured fitness content and your browse experience

I AM INTERESTED IN

Yoga + ——5

Pilates +

Strength +

I WANT TO

Strengthen Muscle +

Burn Fat ✓ ——6

Get Flexible +

TIP If you have some symptoms of a health condition and want to research it yourself, use the Symptom Checker feature of the MSN Health & Fitness app to narrow the search focus for your symptoms.

Checking the weather

Whether you're wandering around your town where you live or visiting another country, being able to anticipate the weather helps you to know what to wear, when to venture out, and how to cope with the vagaries of climate. The Weather app provides information about conditions in your current location or anywhere else of interest to you. You can view weather maps and historical data to spot trends. You can also get news about emerging weather patterns, from a local shower to more threatening conditions such as hurricanes or tornadoes.

This section offers step-by-step advice on how to make the most of the Weather app and use the data it provides to plan your day.

In this section:

- Viewing the current weather
- Adding your favorite places
- Changing your launch location
- Choosing Fahrenheit or Celsius
- Viewing weather maps
- Finding weather news
- Displaying historical weather data

Viewing the current weather

When you want to know what the day or week has in store for you weather-wise, the Weather app can be very useful. When you open the Weather app, you can view the weather information for the default location, or you can select other locations and check the current conditions for them.

View weather details

1 Click the Start button.

2 Click the Weather tile.

3 Drag the scrollbar to view hourly weather details such as precipitation as well as other details like sunrise and sunset, and the phases of the moon.

> **TIP** Here's a shortcut to getting your local weather report. If you have allowed access to your location (in the Action Center, by clicking the Location button), you enable Cortana to reflect the weather where your computer is located. With your Location turned to on, Cortana's main panel then shows you the weather in your current location.

Adding your favorite places

From your home town to the towns where your business has branches or the nearest big city, you might want to include several locations that the Weather app tracks for you on a regular

basis. Weather gives you the ability to designate one default location and an unlimited number of favorite places.

Add a favorite place

1 With the Weather app open, click the Places button.

2 Click the Add button

3 In the Search box, type a city name or postal code.

4 In the results list, click an item.

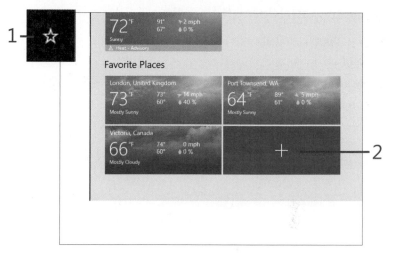

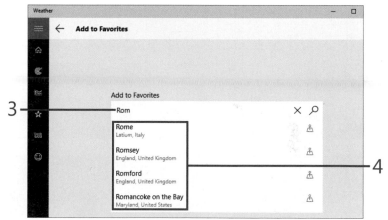

> ✓ **TIP** To remove a location, with Favorite Places displayed, right-click the location, and then, on the shortcut menu that opens, click Remove From Favorites.

Changing your launch location

If you move to another place or are out of town on business for a few months, being able to change your default location—referred to in the Weather app as the *Launch* Location—is convenient. You can manually type your location or allow Windows to detect your current location.

Choose your default location

1 With the Weather app open, click the Places button.

2 Right-click the Launch Location.

3 Click Change Launch Location.

4 In the Default Location box, type a new location.

5 Click the Back button to return to the Weather app home screen.

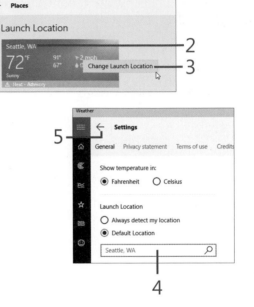

TIP To display a location's weather without adding it to Favorite Places, from the Places window, in the City Or ZIP Code search box, type a location. The weather for that location is displayed, but it isn't added to your Favorite Places.

TIP If you'd rather use your current location as the default location, in the Launch Location settings, click the Always Detect My Location.

Choosing Fahrenheit or Celsius

If you're from Toronto, your temperature measurement of choice is likely Celsius. If you're from New York, Fahrenheit is your familiar measurement. In the Weather app, you can easily change how temperatures are presented to suit your preference.

Make settings for temperature measurements

1 With the Weather app open, click the Places button.

2 Right-click the Launch Location.

3 Click Change Launch Location.

4 Click either the Fahrenheit or Celsius option.

5 Click the Back button to return to the Weather app home screen.

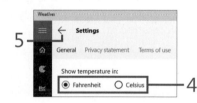

✓ **TIP** When you choose Fahrenheit or Celsius in the Launch Location settings, that's the measurement that will be used for all your Favorite Places, regardless of the preferred measurement standard in that country.

Viewing weather maps

In the Weather app, you can choose to view weather trends on a map. For example, with a weather map, you can move around the country spotting areas of colors that indicate rain or snow.

A legend along the bottom of the Maps window helps you to identify rain, snow, and other weather patterns.

View weather by location on a map

1 With the Weather app open, click Maps.

2 Click the Zoom In or Zoom Out button to view a more or less-detailed map.

3 To move through the last hour of weather, click the Play button.

4 To change locations, in the City Or ZIP Code box, type the new information.

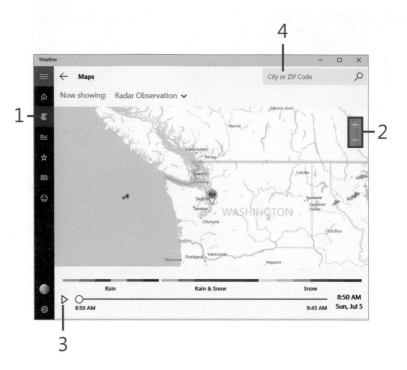

TRY THIS To display different information on the Maps feature of Weather, click the Now Showing drop-down list and choose from Temperature, Radar Observation, Radar Forecast, Precipitation, Satellite, or Cloud.

Finding weather news

News stories about impending weather can provide valuable details about the phenomena headed your way. The News section of the Weather app can produce articles on topics ranging from an upcoming heatwave or snowstorm to global warming.

Read weather news

1   With the Weather app open, click the News button.

2   Drag the scrollbar to move through the stories.

3   Click a story to read it.

Displaying historical weather data

Weather trends can help you to spot the way your year will go, weather-wise, or how the global climate is gradually changing. The Historical Weather feature of the Weather app provides graphs and statistics such as average rainfall and record-high temperatures.

See a graph of weather trends

1 With the Weather app open, click the Historical Weather button.

2 Click a different month in the chart to display historical temperature ranges for that month.

3 Drag the scrollbar to see more information.

4 If you want data for a location other than your Launch Location, in the City Or ZIP Code box, type the new information, and then click a result.

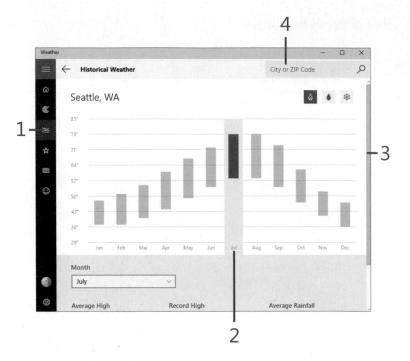

TIP To view trends for temperature, rainfall, or snowfall, in the top-right corner of the Historical Weather window, below the Search box, click the appropriate icon.

Using Maps

19

Using the Windows 10 Maps app, you can view locations around the globe. You can view your current location or any other specific location you're searching for, and then get directions from one location to other. You can take advantage of a variety of views of maps, from Aerial to Road views; Road views can also show traffic problems in real time. You can also use tools to tilt and rotate maps.

In addition, you can use Cortana to designate favorite locations that will then be available in Maps Favorites, and view and manipulate three-dimensional maps of many cities around the world.

In this section:

- Opening Maps and showing your location
- Getting directions in Maps
- Zooming in and out
- Changing map views
- Rotating and tilting maps
- Viewing Favorites
- Viewing cities in 3-D

Opening Maps and showing your location

The Maps app is able to locate where you are in the world and help you to find nearby businesses, such as restaurants, or provide directions. To do this, though, you need to open the Maps app and allow it to find your location.

Find your location in Maps

1 Click the Start button.

2 Click the Maps tile.

3 Click the Maps button.

4 On the toolbar, click the Show My Location button.

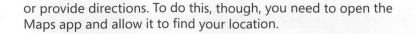

> **TIP** You might have been prompted to turn on location tracking when you first set up Windows or opened the Maps app. If you chose not to do so at that time, you can turn on location-tracking capabilities by clicking the Action Center button, which is located on the taskbar, and then click Location. If you would like to turn off the feature when you're done with it, click Location again.

> **TRY THIS** You can also show your location in Maps by pressing Ctrl+Home.

Getting directions in Maps

People often use maps apps to get from point A to point B. The Maps app in Windows 10 has a very nice directions feature with which you can even generate step-by-step instructions on how to get to your destination along with an accompanying map, or display mileage and time estimates for your trip.

Get directions

1 With the Maps app open, click the Directions button.

2 Click the From box (this might say My Location if you've displayed your location), and then type a start location such as a street address, business name, or city.

3 Click the To box, and then type a destination (you can also select a recent location from the list in this view).

4 Review the displayed directions.

5 If you like, click Go to display a map with step-by-step directions.

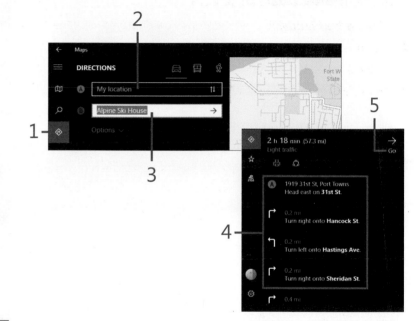

> **TIP** By default, directions are prepared with the assumption that you're traveling by car. To get directions if you're on foot or planning on taking public transit, click the icon with a walker or bus, respectively, which you can find directly above the From box.

> **TRY THIS** While entering start and ending locations in the Directions window, click the Options button and choose what to avoid, such as Traffic, Toll Roads, or Tunnels.

Zooming in and out

The Maps app can give you a broad view of an area or a detailed view of individual streets and landmarks. The Zoom In and Zoom Out feature in Maps helps you to find what you're looking for.

Zoom in and out

1 With the Maps app open and the Maps view displayed, click the Zoom In button.

2 Click the Zoom Out button.

✓ **TIP**   You can use a keyboard shortcut to zoom in or out. To zoom in press Ctrl+Plus Sign. To zoom out press Ctrl+Minus Sign.

→ **TRY THIS**   If you have a touchscreen computer, you can zoom in by putting two fingers together, touching the screen, and then spreading them apart. To zoom out, place your fingers apart on the screen, and then pinch them together.

Changing map views

The Maps app offers two viewing options: Aerial and Road. With each of these views, you can also show or hide a Traffic overlay, which shows traffic problems that you might want to avoid. You can also display details about those traffic problems to help you determine the best route for your travels.

Choose a map view

1 With the Maps app open and displaying a map for a single destination, click the Map Views button.

2 Click the alternate view from that which you're currently viewing; for example click Aerial if you're viewing Traffic, and vice versa.

3 Click the Map Views button, and then click Traffic.

4 Click a traffic warning symbol.

5 Read the details about the traffic condition.

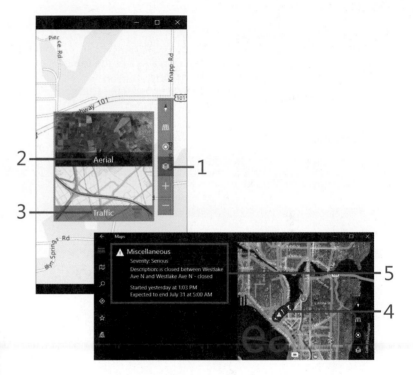

> **TIP** To update maps in the Maps app (to ensure that you're getting the most current information possible), click Settings and then, in the Offline Maps category, verify that Map Updates is set to automatically update maps.

> **TIP** To hide traffic information, click the Map Views button again, and then click Hide Traffic.

Rotating and tilting maps

There are two features of the Maps app that can help you to gain some perspective on what you're viewing. First, you can choose to rotate the map so that North is shown at the top of the map, or rotate the map clockwise or counterclockwise.

Second, you can tilt the map display up or down so that rather than seeing the view as if from directly above, you see it at an angle, and items on the map seem to be fading off into the distance.

Change map angles

1 With the Maps app open and a map displayed, at the top of the toolbar, click the Rotate Map So North Is Up button.

2 Click either the Rotate Counterclockwise or Rotate Clockwise button.

3 Click the Tilt button.

4 Click the Tilt Up or Tilt Down button.

5 To discontinue viewing at an angle, click the Tilt button again.

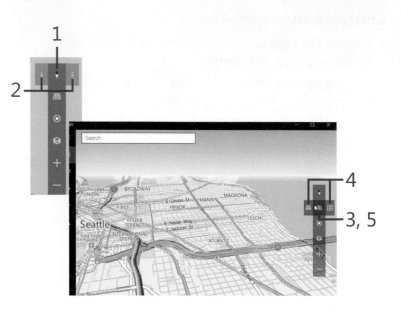

TIP   To further broaden the angle of tilt on a map, click the Tilt Up or Tilt Down control repeatedly (to a maximum of three shifts of tilt). To return to the zero tilt view, click the center Tilt button.

Viewing Favorites

You create favorite places by using Cortana's Notebook. In the About Me settings, you'll find a Favorite Places setting. By editing this, you can add favorite places. The next time you open

the Maps app, when you click the Favorites button in the Navigation bar, you'll find these favorites listed. You can then display directions and information about those favorites.

Display favorite locations

1 With the Maps app open, click the Favorites button.

2 Click a favorite place.

3 Click the Pin To Start button to pin the location to the Start menu.

4 Scroll down to see more information such as hours and reviews.

> **TIP** To delete a Favorite, display Favorites, and then right-click the one that you want to remove. On the shortcut menu that opens, click Delete. This deletes it from both the Maps app and Cortana's Favorites.

Viewing cities in 3-D

With the Maps app, you can display a three-dimensional view of many cities around the world. 3-D views make it possible for you to explore a city from an aerial view. When you display a city in 3-D, you can use the tilt and rotate tools on the right end of the toolbar to manipulate the view.

See select cities in 3-D

1 With the Maps app open, click the 3D Cities button.

2 Click a city.

3 Click the Back arrow to go to the Maps app home screen.

 TIP To restore a map to street view from a 3-D city view, on the right end of the toolbar, click the Map button.

Playing with Xbox games

People have been playing games on computers for many years now. Today, games have added many features such as the ability to play with others online and to track your gaming achievements. In addition, you can use an avatar (an illustration that represents a person) as the persona that you present to other gamers or choose a picture, called a *gamerpic*.

The Xbox app is preinstalled in Windows 10. You don't need to own an Xbox console to play games on your computer using this app. If you do own an Xbox, your gaming achievements will be tracked across your devices.

In this section:

- Buying games
- Adding friends
- Switching between an avatar and a gamerpic
- Playing games
- Inviting friends to play games
- Sending a message to a friend
- Recording game screens

Buying games

There is a wide assortment of computer games out there, from children's games to Solitaire and action games. Some games are free, others you must purchase, but you can obtain both from the Windows Store by using the Xbox app.

Get games

1 Click the Start button.

2 Click the Xbox tile.

3 Click the More button.

4 Click Store.

5 Scroll down to look at suggested games in categories such as Top Free Games or Top Paid Games.

6 Click a game to view details about it.

(continued on next page)

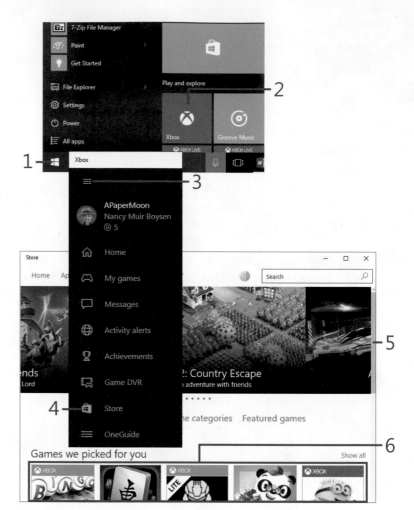

Get games *(continued)*

7   Click the Price button (labeled with either the price of the game or the word "Free").

8   If you're purchasing a game (not downloading a free one), type your account password.

9   Click Sign In.

10 Click Buy.

Disney Checkout Challenge
Disney
★★★★★

Share

Do you have what it takes to climb the ranks from "Checker-in-Training" to "Checkout Chairman"?!? Test out your
More

$0.99

Screenshots

Please reenter your password

Sign in with your Microsoft account. You can use this account with other apps on this device. Learn more.

page7@live.com

Password

Forgot my password

$5.99 plus tax

Buy   Cancel   Sign in

Adding friends

Although you can play games on your own on your computer, in the gaming world you can also add friends with whom you can play online games. After you add friends, you can then invite a friend to play a game, compare achievements, and more.

Add a friend

1 With the Xbox app open, click Friends.

2 Click Favorites.

3 In the Find People box, type a name.

4 Click the Search button.

5 Click Add Friend.

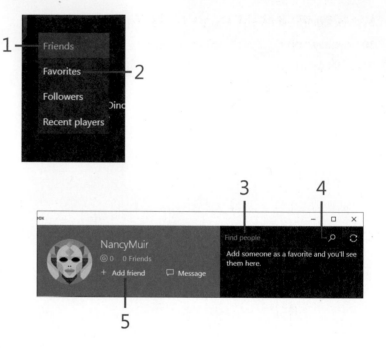

Switching between an avatar and a gamerpic

An avatar is an illustration that represents your gaming persona to others. Xbox offers the option of using an avatar or a *gamerpic*. A gamerpic is a small circle containing an illustration of things such as flowers, dragons, and more. You are assigned an avatar by default, but you can change to a gamerpic with a simple procedure.

Choose an avatar or gamerpic

1 With Xbox open, click your Gamer button.

2 Click Customize.

3 Click Switch To Gamerpic.

4 Click a gamerpic preview.

5 Click Save.

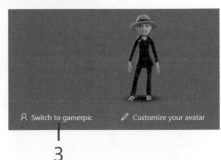

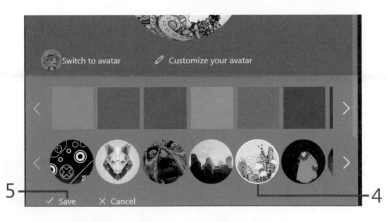

TIP To edit your avatar, you can click Customize Your Avatar in step 3 and download a Microsoft avatar design app.

Switching between an avatar and a gamerpic: Choose an avatar or gamerpic **233**

Playing games

After you own a game, you can begin to play. Of course, games vary widely, from Solitaire to car-racing games, and they all have different features. Still, each game has its own controls and settings, but the basic process of finding and playing a game is the same.

Play a game

1 With Xbox open, click the More button.

2 Click My Games.

3 Click Play adjacent to a game to play it.

 TIP To stop playing a game if it opens in a separate window, in the top-right corner of the window, click the Close button.

Inviting friends to play games

Even though playing a game on your own can be fun, some-times it's more fun to play against an opponent. After you've added friends who have the same game you have, you can invite them to play with you via an online connection.

Invite a friend to play

1 With Xbox open, click the More button.

2 Click your Gamer button.

3 Click the Friends button

4 Click a friend to display details.

5 Click Invite.

6 In the message box that opens, click OK to confirm the invitation. Your friend receives an email and can then click to join the game.

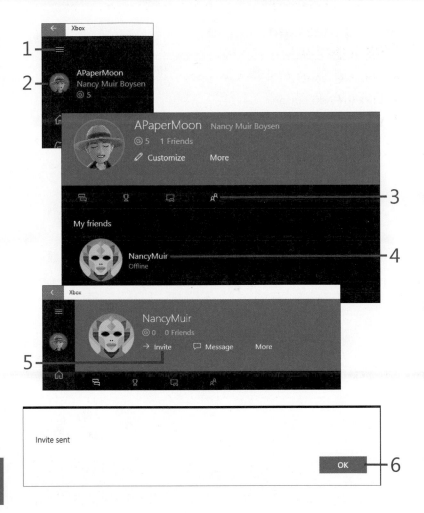

TIP You can choose to play a game or to start a party, which involves a session with several players.

Sending a message to a friend

Having gamer friends makes your gaming experience richer. You can even use tools in Xbox to communicate with your friends, sending them messages about getting together for a game or to boast about your latest scores.

Send a message

1 With Xbox open, click the More button.

2 Click Messages.

3 Click the Add button.

4 Click the To box, and then select a friend.

(continued on next page)

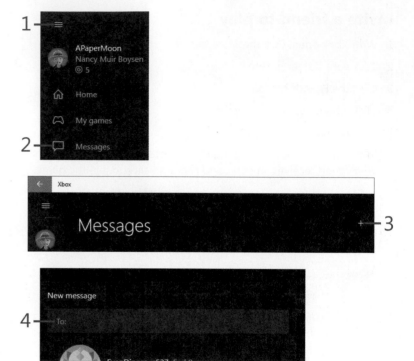

Send a message *(continued)*

5 When you're finished adding addresses, click Done.

6 In the Reply box, type a reply.

7 Click Send.

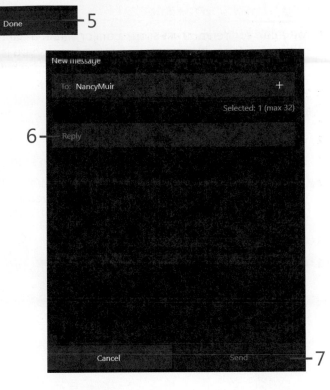

Recording game screens

If you think you're about to score a major win in a game, you might want to record your gaming session and share it with like-minded gamers. Recording is easy to do, and it helps you to improve your scores over time by viewing your past mistakes and achievements.

Record and share games

1 Play a game in Xbox.

2 While you're playing the game, press the Windows logo key+Alt+R to begin recording; a recording counter displays.

3 Press the Windows logo key+Alt+R again to stop recording.

4 Click the More button.

5 Click the Game DVR button.

6 Click a recording to play it.

 TIP   When you play a recording, you can use editing tools to trim or rename the clip, and then share it with others.

Adding and working with other devices

Windows 10 can work with various devices such as printers, smart TVs, and Bluetooth-enabled peripherals (e.g., a mouse or keyboard). To do this, you need to configure certain settings and connections, which often involves following the guided instructions in something called a *wizard*. For example, you can specify settings to manage the attributes and capabilities of a printer or scanner, or connected devices such as a mouse. You can also examine the properties of devices by using Device Manager and update *device drivers* (small software programs by which Windows 10 connects to and communicates with various devices).

If you no longer need to have a device connected to your computer, you can remove it and its driver software.

In this section:

- Adding a connected device
- Adding a printer or scanner
- Making printer settings
- Using Bluetooth devices
- Viewing device properties in Device Manager
- Updating device drivers
- Removing a device

Adding a connected device

When you connect a device such as a wireless mouse or smart TV, Windows 10 might automatically recognize the device. But in some situations, you might need to manually add the device.

Windows first detects the device and then takes you through steps to set it up.

Set up a connected device

1 Click the Start button.

2 Click Settings.

3 Click Devices.

4 Click Connected Devices.

5 Click Add A Device.

6 In the Add Devices panel, click the name of the device that you want to add.

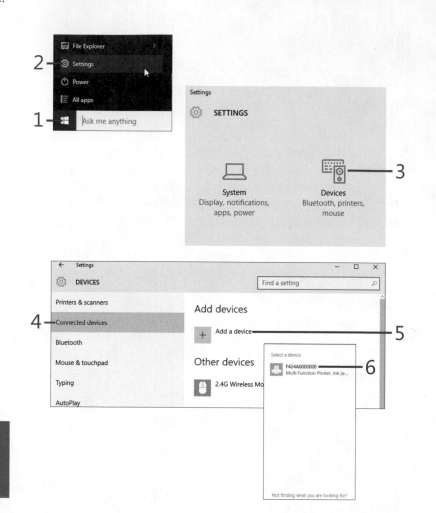

> **TIP** To avoid data download charges when you're connected to a metered connection (one for which you are charged for certain data downloads), in the Connected Devices panel, scroll down and turn off the Download Over Metered Connections setting.

Adding a printer or scanner

Windows 10 provides a unique procedure for adding printers and scanners through the Devices portion of Settings. Windows usually detects printers or scanners through a connected network or physical connection; if it doesn't, you can manually add a device.

Add a printer

1 With the Devices settings window open and Printers & Scanners selected in the left pane, click Add A Printer Or Scanner.

2 In the list that appears, click the printer that you want to add.

3 Click Add Device.

TIP If the printer you want to add doesn't appear in the Add A Printer results, click The Printer That I Want Isn't Listed, and then follow instructions to locate older printers (ones that don't have plug-and-play technology through which Windows can identify them) or provide more information to help Windows locate the printer.

Making printer settings

There are several settings that you can configure when printing a document from within an application. For example, you can select the printer to which you want to print, choose which pages in the document to print, set up page collation, page orientation, and margins. The settings you can make vary depending on the printer that you're using.

Choose how to print

1   In the Cortana search box, type **WordPad**.

2   Press Enter to open the selected app.

(continued on next page)

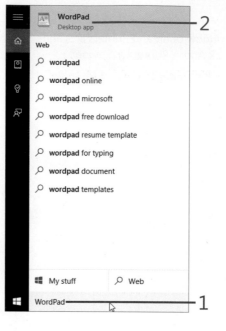

Choose how to print (continued)

3 Click File.

4 Click Print.

5 In the Print dialog box that opens, click Pages and specify a page range; for example, type **3-5**.

6 In the Number Of Copies box, click the up or down arrows or type a number directly in the box to set the number of copies.

7 Select the Collate check box to turn that feature on or off (this only works if you've selected two or more copies in the preceding step).

8 Click Print.

TIP If you print a document to OneNote, you essentially send a copy of it to the online document management system where you can then work with it or share it.

TRY THIS To make further printer settings in the Print dialog box, click the Preferences button. Depending on your printer's features, you can choose options such as the size of paper to print on, print quality, color settings, and so on.

Using Bluetooth devices

Bluetooth is a technology with which you can connect one Bluetooth-enabled device to another when they are within close proximity. For example, you might connect to your smartphone or a Bluetooth keyboard. To use Bluetooth, you must make the device *discoverable* and then pair your computer with it.

Pair your computer with a Bluetooth device

1 Click the Start button.

2 Click Settings.

3 Click Devices.

4 Click Bluetooth.

5 Click the Bluetooth switch to turn the feature on if it's off.

6 Click a recognized Bluetooth device to pair it with your computer.

7 Click Pair.

> **TIP** Bluetooth works within an approximate range of 30 feet (10 meters). If you need to connect with devices at a greater distance, you might try to use a Wi-Fi–enabled device and add it to a Wi-Fi network.

Viewing device properties in Device Manager

Device Manager is a Windows feature that makes it possible for you to view all devices connected to or installed on your computer, such as a keyboard or graphics controller, and examine their properties. Being able to access this information can help you to troubleshoot problems with your computer.

View information about your devices

1 From the Devices settings window with Printers & Scanners selected, in the Related Settings section, click Device Manager.

2 Double-click a category such as Keyboards.

3 Right-click a device.

4 On the shortcut menu that opens, click Properties.

5 Click various tabs to view details about the device.

6 Click OK to close the dialog box.

> ✓ **TIP** When you click a device, tools appear above the device window. You can click the Property button there to display the device properties as an alternative to the right-click method described in this task.

Updating device drivers

To connect devices to your computer, you must install *device drivers*. These small programs give Windows the information it needs to communicate with the devices and provide the appropriate instructions to them. Device drivers are regularly updated to improve their functionality or add security features. For that reason it's useful to know how to update your drivers.

Search for updated driver software

1 With Device Manager window open (see the previous task), right-click a device.

2 On the shortcut menu that opens, click Update Driver Software.

3 Click Search Automatically For Updated Driver Software.

4 Click the device model for which you want the updated driver.

5 Click Next to install the new driver.

TIP If you believe the device driver software might be located on your computer or a storage drive, in step 3 you can click Browse My Computer For Driver Software.

Removing a device

If you are no longer using a device, you might want to remove it from your computer. This makes lists of available devices shorter so that you can more easily manage active devices, and it removes unneeded driver software from your computer, freeing up memory.

Remove a device from your computer

1 With the Device Manager window open, right-click the name of the device that you want to remove.

2 On the shortcut menu that opens, click Uninstall.

3 Click OK to confirm that you want to remove the device.

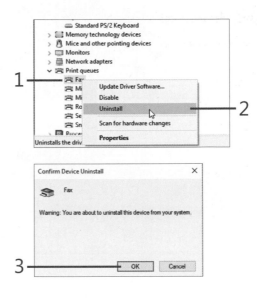

Working with OneDrive

In this section:

- Navigating OneDrive
- Creating a new folder
- Uploading files to OneDrive
- Searching for a file in OneDrive
- Creating documents with Office Online
- Sharing folders
- Renaming files and folders
- Deleting files and folders

Microsoft OneDrive is an online service for storing content and sharing that content with others. When you first set up Windows 10, you'll be asked to also set up OneDrive, which requires you to be signed-in with your Microsoft account.

OneDrive is integrated into apps such as Microsoft Outlook and Office 365, and even mobile apps for Windows smartphones so that you can save documents directly to it and access your content from different devices. With Windows 10, you have a version of OneDrive on your computer and another online version that synchronizes (backs up) your content to the cloud on a regular basis when you go online.

You can go to OneDrive online and create folders, upload content, share that content, and search through it. You can also remove content from OneDrive. With a Microsoft account you can get to OneDrive through Outlook.com, or you can go to *onedrive.live.com* to work with your files.

The first time you go to OneDrive, you need to follow a few simple steps to configure and activate your OneDrive account.

Navigating OneDrive

You access the version of OneDrive stored on your computer as a folder in File Explorer, where you can store documents ready to synchronize with the online version of OneDrive. The real work of sharing and managing files with OneDrive is handled online, where you can access your content from any computer, tablet, or smartphone, from anywhere.

Navigate features of OneDrive

1 With a browser open and Windows signed-in to your account, in the address bar, type **onedrive.live.com**, and then press Enter.

2 Click a folder to display its contents.

3 Click the Back button.

4 Click the Menu button.

5 Click Photos.

6 Drag the scroll bar to view additional photos.

7 Click the Back button.

8 Click Sort.

9 Click the appropriate criteria for sorting, such as Size.

> ✓ **TIP** When you click the Menu button, you see any computers that have access to your OneDrive listed at the bottom of the menu that's displayed.

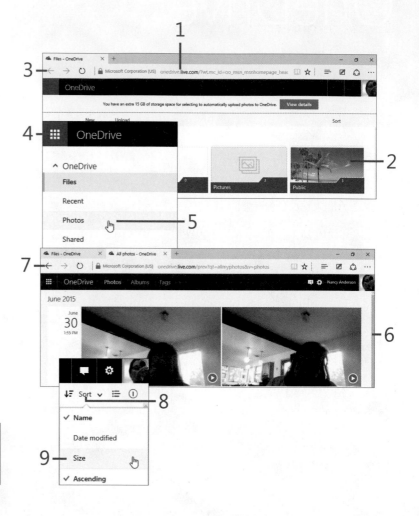

Creating a new folder

Rather than working with folders that are automatically backed up to OneDrive from your computer, you can create a new folder in OneDrive and then upload files to it. This way, you can create your own folders of content online that don't necessarily replicate what's stored on your computer.

Create a folder in OneDrive

1 With the OneDrive open, click New.

2 Click Folder.

3 Type a folder name.

4 Click Create.

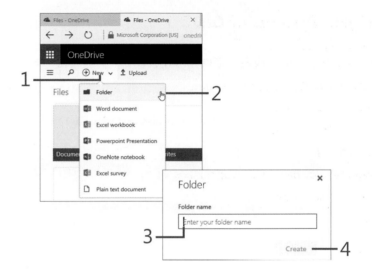

✓ **TIP** If you type a name that already exists in OneDrive, when you click Create in step 4, you'll see a message asking you to try a different name.

Uploading files to OneDrive

Although your Windows 10 computer automatically backs up content to OneDrive, there might be times when you want to upload specific content to an online folder to share it with others. For example, you might want to create a folder called "Third-Quarter Budget" in OneDrive and only upload to it those spreadsheets and other documents that pertain to the third quarter, even though no such folder exists on your computer.

Upload a file or folder

1 With OneDrive open, click a folder or create a new folder (see the previous task).

2 Click Upload.

3 In the Open dialog box, locate the file or files that you want to upload.

4 Click Open.

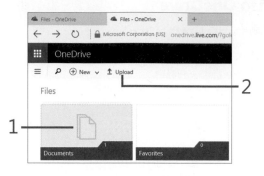

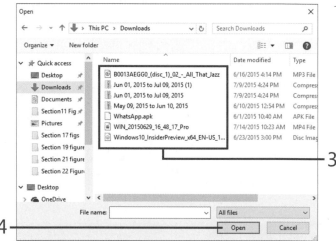

> **TIP** OneDrive comes with 15 GB of free storage (if you subscribe to Office 365, the limit is 1 TB), but you can buy more. On the OneDrive title bar, click the Settings button (the cog icon) and choose Options. Then, click the Buy More Storage button and follow the directions to acquire more storage. Note that you can also get more storage by referring somebody to OneDrive and through various loyalty and app-related promotions.

Searching for a file in OneDrive

When you have many files and folders in OneDrive online, you need a method to search for the specific items you want, just as File Explorer helps you to find content on your computer's hard disk and storage drives. OneDrive offers a Search feature that you can use to do just that.

Search for content

1 With OneDrive open, click the Search button.

2 In the Search box, type a word or phrase, and then press Enter.

3 In the search results, click a file or folder.

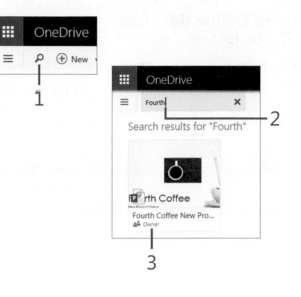

TIP   To change views from a graphic representation of files and folders to a simple list, on the far right of the Search box, click the View button.

Creating documents with Office Online

From within OneDrive, you can create documents that are saved there using Office Online. This suite includes Microsoft Word, Excel, and PowerPoint. You can also create OneNote Notebooks, Excel Surveys, and Plain Text documents. This capability can be very handy when you're using a computer or tablet that doesn't have Office apps installed.

Create a Word Online document

1 With OneDrive open, click New.

2 Click Word Document.

3 Type your document contents.

4 Use the tools on the various tabs to format and organize your content.

5 Click File.

(continued on next page)

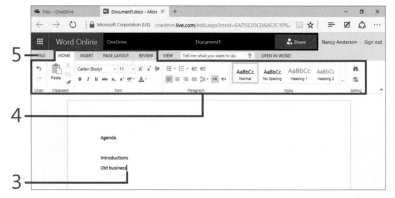

Create a Word Online document *(continued)*

6 Click Save As.

7 Click Save As to save the document to OneDrive.

8 Click the folder where you want to save the file.

9 Click Save.

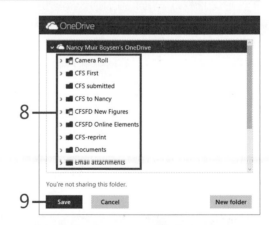

✓ TIP Explore other Save As options to download a copy of the document to your computer or download it to your computer as a PDF file.

Sharing folders

One of the most useful aspects of OneDrive is the ability to share large files with others. Because email attachments are often limited by file size, sharing by using a service such as OneDrive makes it possible for you to share files that you otherwise could not send by email. You share by inviting people via an email to view the file. When you do, you can choose whether those people can simply view the files or actually edit them.

Share OneDrive content with others

1 With OneDrive online open and a folder whose contents you want to share open, click Share.

2 Type an email address.

3 Add a note if you like.

4 Click Recipients Can Edit if you want to give the people with whom you're sharing permission to edit content.

5 Click Share.

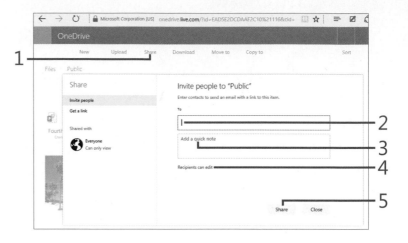

 TIP If you'd rather create your own email and embed a link to your files, in the left panel of the Share window, click Get A Link, and then click the Create link button. Copy and paste the link into your email.

Renaming files and folders

Just as you find it useful to rename files and folders in File Explorer, so you might need to do the same in OneDrive. As project names, company names, and more items change in your life, the ability to rename content in your online storage service helps you to keep up to date.

Rename a file or folder

1 Locate a file or folder in OneDrive and right-click it.

2 On the shortcut menu that opens, click Rename.

3 Type a new name.

4 Click Rename.

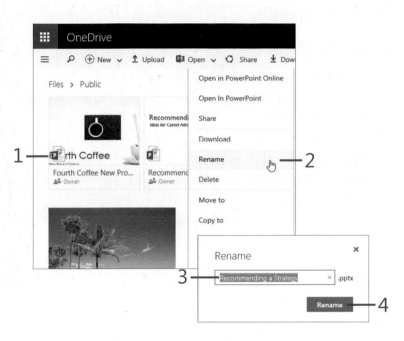

✓ **TIP** You can't rename a file or folder with a name that's already in use. You must use unique names when renaming files or folders.

Deleting files and folders

Although at 15 GB your OneDrive basic storage is impressive, you might find that it fills up faster than you thought it would. To save space you can periodically delete files and folders that you no longer need to save.

Delete content

1 With OneDrive open, in the top-right corner of one or more files or folders that you want to remove, select the round check mark.

2 Click Delete.

3 If you change your mind about deleting the item or items, in the confirmation message that appears, click Undo.

TIP To see how much storage you have available, in OneDrive online, click the Settings button. Click Options, and then select the Storage option. In the right panel, your storage plan and any additional storage are listed. The storage available is listed at the top of this screen.

Maintaining and protecting your computer

Windows 10 provides several handy tools to help keep your computer performing optimally and with the most up-to-date security. You can perform a disk cleanup to remove bits of data that are no longer being used, including temporary files. When you instruct Windows 10 to optimize your hard disk, it takes noncontiguous pieces—or, fragments—and organizes them to make it easier for Windows to locate items, which improves your computer's performance. (Note that if your computer is equipped with a solid-state drive, you won't run into these issues.)

You can perform regular updates to ensure that you have the most current security features for Windows 10 to protect your computer. In addition, you can configure Windows Defender and Windows Firewall, features that help protect your computer and data. If you're experiencing serious problems with your computer, you can reset it to an earlier version of Windows or restore factory settings—settings that were in place when you purchased your computer or upgraded the operating system.

Finally, Location tracking is turned on by default in Windows 10, but you might prefer to turn off this feature to prevent thieves from knowing where your computer is.

In this section:

- Optimizing your hard disk
- Using Disk Cleanup
- Obtaining updates
- Resetting your computer
- Working with Windows Defender
- Running Windows Defender updates and scans
- Configuring Windows Firewall
- Changing Location settings

Optimizing your hard disk

When you save documents, pictures, and so on, Windows 10 stores them on your hard disk in bits and pieces that might or might not be contiguous. That is, pieces of data that make up your report on bird migration patterns might be located all over your drive. Every time you open the document, Windows must look across your entire hard disk to reassemble all these file fragments. Optimizing helps to improve your computer's performance by organizing these pieces such that they are contiguous on your hard drive, and therefore quicker to access.

Run the optimization process

1 In the Cortana Search box, type **optimize**.

2 Click Defragment And Optimize Drives.

3 Click the drive that you want to optimize. This is typically, Windows (C:).

4 Click Optimize.

5 When the status shows that the optimize process is complete, click Close.

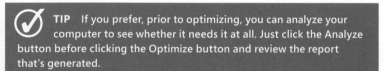

> **TIP** If you prefer, prior to optimizing, you can analyze your computer to see whether it needs it at all. Just click the Analyze button before clicking the Optimize button and review the report that's generated.

> **TIP** You can click Change Settings in the Optimize Drives dialog box and set a scheduled optimization on certain drives at a regular time interval, such as every week.

Using Disk Cleanup

When you use your computer for various tasks, your hard disk begins to fill up with lots of information that could be in the form of files, temporary files created as you browse the Internet, old software programs, and so on. Disk Cleanup looks for corrupt data, temporary files, and unused bits and pieces on your hard disk and deletes them, freeing up space that you could be using for other things.

Clear up space by using Disk Cleanup

1 In the Settings search box, type **Disk Cleanup**, and then press Enter.

2 Click Free Up Disk Space By Deleting Unnecessary Files.

3 Select the check boxes to the left of any types of files or folders that you want to remove.

4 Click Clean Up System Files.

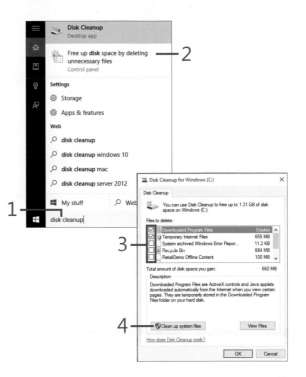

 TIP If you're concerned that Disk Cleanup might delete files you need, you can view the files that Windows suggests and clear the check mark (deselect) for those that you don't want removed before proceeding. To examine the files, in the Disk Cleanup For Windows dialog box, click the View Files button.

Obtaining updates

Microsoft makes updates available from time to time to fix bugs or security gaps created by the latest attack technique used to infiltrate your computer. It's important to get these updates to protect your computer and data. With Windows 10, which will rely on frequent changes to add or modify app features as well as its operating system, updating becomes even more important. Windows automatically checks for updates on a regular basis, but you also can manually check if you prefer.

Run Windows Update

1 In Settings, click Update & Security.

2 With Windows Update settings displayed, click Check For Updates.

3 Windows searches for and installs any updates; click Install Now to complete the update.

TIP When updates are performed, Windows often restarts to finalize the changes. If you are bothered by your computer restarting with little notice, under Windows Updates click the Advanced Options link. Then, at the top of the next window that opens, click the drop-down list and choose Notify To Schedule Restart.

Resetting your computer

When you experience serious problems with your computer and you see no way to solve them, you might need to reset your computer. With the reset process, you can choose whether you want to retain your files or get rid of them, and then you can reinstall Windows. Resetting can remove apps you've installed or revert any settings that you've configured that might have corrupted Windows, and thus you start with a clean slate.

Repair problems with a reset

1   In the Update & Security window of Settings, click Recovery.

2   In the Reset This PC section, click Get Started.

3   Click a box to select the option you want for your reset.

Your options are:

- Keep all your files

- Remove everything, including files, apps, and settings

- Restore your computer to factory settings (assuming that you aren't already on a clean factory-setting version of Windows)

TIP   If you decide to reset your computer, consider backing up all your files on an external storage device such as a USB stick, or saving them to the cloud. If you are removing apps, also ensure that you have a way to reinstall those that you need after the reset, either from DVDs or the Internet.

Working with Windows Defender

Today, there are many situations in which you can unintentionally install malware on a computer, which can damage its contents or spy on the activities of the user. You can buy third-party security applications, but your first line of defense is to use the antimalware program built in to Windows 10 called Windows

Defender. You can turn off Windows Defender (though it's not recommended); if you do, after a period of time, Windows will turn it on again because it's that important that you have this protection.

Manage Windows Defender settings

1 With Update & Security selected in Settings, in the left panel, click Windows Defender.

2 Click the Real-Time Protection switch if it's set to Off.

3 Scroll down to the Exclusions section, and then click the Add An Exclusion link.

(continued on next page)

Manage Windows Defender settings (continued)

4 Click the Add button for a type of exclusion such as Files or Folders.

5 Locate the Item to exclude.

6 Click Exclude This File.

7 Click the Close button.

TIP If you find an instance of malware on your computer, you can help make Windows Defender stronger by sending a sample to Microsoft. To do so, in the Windows Defender settings, ensure that the Sample Submission feature is set to on.

Running Windows Defender updates and scans

After you turn on Windows Defender, it will protect your computer automatically. However, if you want to run a manual update of virus definitions and scan—for example, to determine if you have visited a questionable website or downloaded a suspicious file—you can do so in the Windows Defender app.

Run manual updates and scans

1 With the Update & Security settings window open, in the left panel, click Windows Defender, scroll to the bottom of the right panel, and then click the Use Windows Defender link.

2 Click the Update tab.

3 Click Update to obtain the latest definitions before running a scan.

4 Click the Home tab.

5 Click a scan option.

6 Click Scan Now.

7 Click the Close button.

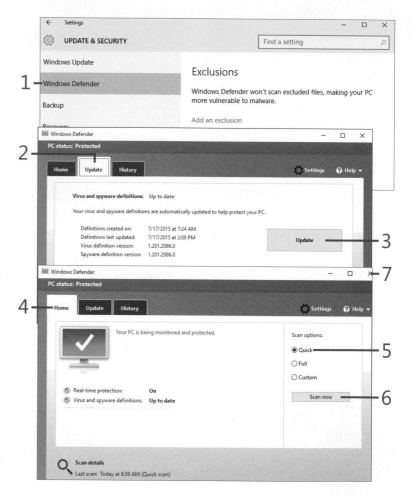

> **TIP** You can access the Windows Defender app by clicking the Show Hidden Icons button in the Notifications area of the taskbar, clicking the PC Status button, and then clicking Open.

Configuring Windows Firewall

A firewall is a tool that stops suspicious software from being downloaded to your computer when you go online. A firewall acts like a barrier between your computer and the Internet, but you can set up exclusions to allow certain content to download.

Windows Firewall is built in to Windows 10. Note that these steps apply to a home network; if you are working on a company network, your administrator will deal with firewall settings for all users.

Protect your computer by using Windows Firewall

1 In the Cortana search box, type **Windows Firewall**.

2 Click Windows Firewall.

3 Click Turn Windows Firewall On Or Off.

4 In the Private Network Settings section, click to turn Windows Firewall on if it's off.

5 In the Public Network Settings section, click to turn Windows Firewall on if it's off.

6 Click OK.

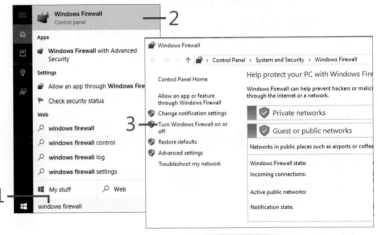

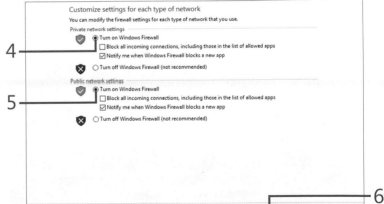

> ✓ **TIP**   If you are using a third-party security product, it might have overridden Windows Firewall with its own firewall feature. If you prefer to use Windows Firewall, examine the settings for the security product's to learn how to turn off its firewall.

Changing Location settings

It's possible for certain applications to locate you geographically. Sometimes this is helpful, as with the Maps app that can provide directions from your current location to a destination (for more information on this app, read Section 19, "Using Maps"). However, some apps use your location to sell you items, and some criminals use your location for identity theft or to commit offline crimes, including stealing your computer itself. If you prefer, you can change your Location settings so that your computer's whereabouts are not visible to others.

Choose to share your location or not

1 In Settings, click Privacy.

2 Click Location.

3 Under Location For This Device Is On (or Off) click the Change button.

4 Click the Location For This Device switch to change the current setting, if you want.

5 To stop apps and services from asking for your location, in the Privacy window, click the Location switch to On, if it's not already.

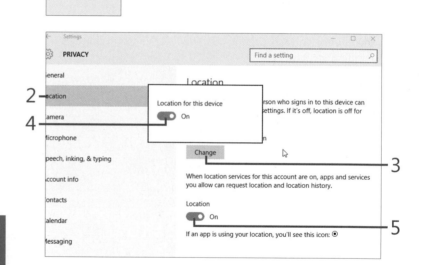

> ✓ **TIP**   To quickly turn Location services off, click the Action Center button, and then click the Location button. Repeat this procedure to turn it on again.

> → **TRY THIS**   To allow only certain apps to request your location, scroll down in the Privacy window, and then, in the Choose Apps That Can Use Your Location section, click any of the on/off switches to allow requests (on) or deny requests (off).

Troubleshooting

24

In this section:

- Searching for help by using Cortana
- Using Task Manager
- Restoring your system to an earlier time
- Getting help from Get Started
- Getting remote assistance
- Using Advanced Startup

Everybody has experienced computer troubles at one time or another. It might have been something as minor as a piece of software that freezes a computer, or perhaps you've encountered a more worrisome system failure. Windows 10 has many built-in tools that you can use to solve these problems and get your computer back on track, such as System Restore to restore your computer to an earlier time when it was functioning well; Remote Assistance to allow another person to take over and fix your computer; and Task Manager, which you can use to exit an app that's become nonresponsive.

In addition, you can find help with your problems with the Get Started app, which is like a high-tech user manual that provides information about a variety of Windows 10 settings and features. You can also search for help by using Cortana to assist you in locating settings on your computer, or online articles and blogs about a topic that might help you by learning from other users' experiences.

Searching for help by using Cortana

To a great extent, Cortana has become your new help system in Windows 10. Using Cortana, you can search for a setting on your computer or search online for help from articles and Microsoft documentation. In addition, you can scan blogs where you might find the answer you need posted by a Microsoft expert or another user. To have Cortana respond to voice commands using the "Hey Cortana" greeting, click to open the Cortana panel, and then, in the tools on the left, click Notebook. Click Settings and then click the Hey Cortana setting to On.

Find help by using Cortana

1 Click the Cortana search box, and then type a word or phrase.

2 Click an item in the results to open a setting or view web content.

3 Say, "Hey Cortana," or click the Microphone button, and then ask a question such as, "How do I restart Windows?"

4 View the results either in the Cortana panel or on the web.

> **TIP** When you search for help by using Cortana, she searches using the Bing search engine. Very often it's important that you get the most current information because technology changes so quickly (you don't want results about Windows 7 when you're trying to find information about Windows 10, for example). If you click the Web button in the Cortana search box, you can then use the drop-down list at the top of the search results in Bing, which, by default, is labeled Any Time. You can then choose a timeframe, such as Past 24 Hours, Past Month, or Past Week, to narrow your search results.

Using Task Manager

When you are working with Windows 10, a setting or app can become nonresponsive. You might find that you're no longer able to make a choice or type text or close the window, which makes it impossible to proceed or even use any other settings or apps. When that happens, you can use Task Manager to exit the nonresponsive app and get back to work.

Use Task Manager to exit a nonresponsive program

1 On your keyboard, press Ctrl+Alt+Del.

2 Click Task Manager.

3 Click a running app.

4 Click End Task.

5 Click the Close button.

Restoring your system to an earlier time

With Windows 10, you can create a *restore point*, which is a point in time at which you saved your computer's settings (and everything was running smoothly). If you experience problems later, perhaps after installing a new app or changing your settings, going back to a time before that change could solve problems. Before you can create a restore point, you must turn on system protection for a drive.

Create a restore point

1 In Cortana's search box, type the words **restore point**.

2 In the results, click Create A Restore Point.

3 Click Create.

4 In the text box, type a name or description for the restore point.

5 Click Create, and then, when the process is complete, click the Close button in the confirmation that appears (not shown).

TIP To turn on system protection for a computer drive, in the System Properties dialog box, on the System Protection tab, click the Configure button. In the Restore Settings section that opens, select the Turn On System Protection option, and then click OK.

TRY THIS After creating a restore point, if you experience problems, go to the System Properties dialog box shown in step 4, and then click the System Restore button. Follow the instructions, selecting the restore point you want to use and confirming the system restore.

Getting help from Get Started

When you encounter a problem or can't figure out how to accomplish something, you can turn to the Get Started app. This built-in app is like a constantly updated user manual for Windows 10. A series of articles with images and links to additional information are categorized into topics such as "Setting Things Up" and "Cortana." You can also go to the "What's New" feature of Get Started to see an overview of new features in Windows 10.

Using Get Started

1 Click the Start button.

2 Click All Apps.

3 Scroll down and click Get Started.

4 On the left, click a category, and then read the article.

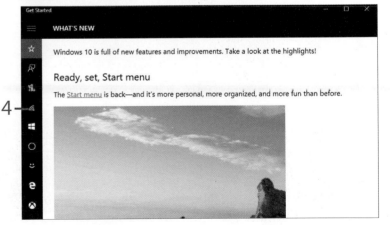

> ✓ **TIP** Get Started includes some topics other than Windows 10 settings. To learn more about the new Microsoft Edge browser visit that section of Get Started. There are also sections on the Xbox app and Microsoft Office.

Getting remote assistance

Sometimes, all you need when you encounter a problem is a little help. Perhaps you have a more computer-savvy friend or workplace associate who has offered to lend a hand, and, conveniently, she doesn't even need to be standing next to you to render assistance. Instead, you can assign her access to

your computer from a remote location and let her view your computer screen, helping you to make changes to settings that might solve your problem. Note that you must turn off Windows Firewall to allow remote access to your computer.

Get help from another user

1   In the Cortana Search box, type **invite someone to help you**.

2   In the results, click Invite Someone To Connect To Your PC And Help You.

3   Click Invite Someone You Trust To Help You.

4   Click Save This Invitation As A File.

(continued on next page)

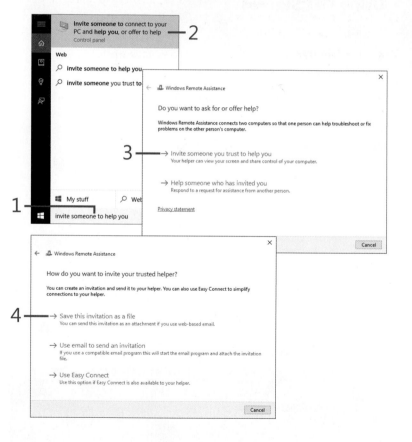

Get help from another user *(continued)*

5 Find the location to which you want to save the invitation.

6 Modify the File Name if you like.

7 Click Save, and then email the file to the other person.

8 Provide your helper with the password that appears.

9 When that person opens the email attachment and types the password, a message will appear on your screen asking if you'd like to allow access. Click Yes.

10 When you and your helper have finished your session, click Stop Sharing.

> ⚠ **CAUTION** Be sure that you know and trust the person to whom you give access. Anybody who you let use your computer via remote access can go anywhere and view anything on your computer, including personally sensitive information. Also, remember to turn on Windows Firewall again after you complete your session.

Using Advanced Startup

If you're having a serious computer problem, sometimes rebooting your computer—that is, turning it off and then on again—can resolve it. However, if the system files your computer uses to restart are damaged, you might need to use

another method to start up. One option is to use backup system files that you stored on a USB stick or DVD. To do that, you need to use the Advanced Startup feature to restart your computer.

Choose to startup from external storage

1 With the external storage that contains the system files connected to your computer, from the Settings window choose Update & Security.

2 In the left panel, click Recovery.

3 In the Advanced Startup section, click Restart Now.

4 On the screen that appears, click Use A Device, and then choose a device from the list that appears (not shown).

TIP By selecting the Troubleshoot option instead of Use A Device, you can access advanced options for troubleshooting your computer problems.

Appendix

Taking advantage of Windows 10 keyboard shortcuts

People tend to interact with their computers in different ways. Some like using a touchscreen. Others live by their mouse. And still others prefer to turn to their keyboard to get most things done. Keyboard shortcuts provide a handy way to accomplish a great many actions by using keystroke combinations such as Ctrl+X to cut selected text from a document or Ctrl+Shift+Esc to call up the Task Manager.

In Windows 10, there are shortcuts that you might be familiar with and some new shortcuts for accessing new features such as Action Center, Task View, and Settings. Here's a rundown of some of the most useful keyboard shortcuts for Windows 10.

Windows logo key+I	Open Settings
Windows logo key+D	Add a desktop
Windows logo key+Ctrl+F4	Close current desktop
Windows logo key+Tab	Open Task View
Windows logo key	Open or close the Start menu
Windows logo key+L	Go to the Lock screen
Windows logo key+Q	Open Cortana
Windows logo key+C	Open Cortana in listening mode
Windows logo key+A	Open Action Center
Windows logo key+E	Open File Explorer
Windows logo key+X	Display the desktop menu
Windows logo key+D	Go to the desktop
F1	Open Help
Alt+Tab	Switch among open programs
Windows logo key+H	Open Share panel
Windows logo key+K	Open Connect panel for wireless devices

Shortcuts for editing

Ctrl+C	Copy
Ctrl+X	Cut
Ctrl+V	Paste
Ctrl+B	Bold
Ctrl+U	Underline
Ctrl+I	Italic
Ctrl+Z	Undo last edit or entry
Ctrl+A	Select active window items
Shift+Left	Moves cursor one space to the left
Shift+Right	Moves cursor one space to the right
Shift+Up arrow	Moves cursor to previous line
Shift+Down arrow	Moves cursor to next line

Accessibility shortcuts

Windows logo key+U	Open Ease of Access Center
Shift (five times)	Turn StickyKeys on or off
Left Alt+Left Shift+Num Lock	Toggle MouseKeys on or off
Left Alt+Left Shift+Print Screen	Turn high contrast on or off

Windows logo key+M	Minimize all open windows
Tab	Move to next item in a dialog box
Shift+Tab	Move to the previous item in a dialog box
Esc	Cancel an action
Ctrl+Shift+Esc	Open Task Manager
Windows logo key+Left arrow	Snap current window to the left side of the screen
Windows logo key+Right arrow	Snap current window to the right side of the screen
Windows logo key+Up arrow	Snap current window to the top of the screen
Windows logo key+Down arrow	Snap current window to the bottom of the screen
Alt+Enter	Display properties for an object selected in File Explorer

Glossary

A

Action Center   A panel that you display by clicking the Action Center button on the taskbar. The Action Center includes Notifications and quick settings buttons.

Active window   The currently selected window.

Administrator   A user account with administrative privileges such as the ability to modify security and other user settings.

All Apps   A selection in the Start menu that displays all of the apps that are installed on your computer in an alphabetical list.

App   An application that provides the ability to perform a certain function such as currency conversion or playing media.

Application   An application that provides more complex functionality than an app, such as a word processor or spreadsheet.

B

BCC   Blind carbon copy. A way to send a copy of an email to a recipient without other recipients knowing.

Box   Also referred to as a text box, this is a field in a form or dialog box in which you type text.

Browse   To use a web browser app to look for content online. Also, to browse for a drive or folder on a computer, as in File Explorer.

C

CC   Carbon copy. A way to send a copy to an additional recipient or recipients when creating, forwarding, or responding to an email.

Click   To place your mouse cursor on a selected object and click the left mouse button to perform an action.

Cloud   Refers to a storage shared pool of content, apps, and documents that can be accessed from any computer, rather than being stored locally on a computer or private network.

Command   An option on a menu, such as Open or Save.

Compress   To shrink the contents of a file by encoding it with an algorithm in order to store or share that file through media with limited storage capability, such as an email attachment.

Control Panel   The interface for accessing certain advanced settings.

Cookie   A small file installed on a user's computer by a website to track that user's online activities. Cookies can be used by legitimate businesses to better serve return customers, but they also can be used for less legitimate purposes.

Cortana   A personal assistant feature in Windows 10 with which you can search your computer or the web, and instruct your computer to take actions such as opening an app or creating a reminder by voice or typing.

Cursor　A blinking line on a computer screen that indicates the active location within text in a document.

Cut　The act of cutting an object or text from a document which removes it from that document and places it on the Windows Clipboard; you can then paste it into another location if you wish.

D

Defragment　A procedure that takes pieces of files that have become separated and stored in various locations on a hard disk and arranges them in contiguous blocks. This makes it faster for a computer to find and access that content.

Desktop　The main interface in Windows 10 that displays active apps, shortcuts to apps and content, and a taskbar for accessing apps and various settings. In Windows 10 you can create multiple desktops that include their own active apps.

Details pane　A pane in File Explorer that displays details about a selected file or folder.

Dialog box　A window that's displayed when accessing certain settings. Dialog boxes typically contain text boxes, drop-down lists, various selections and options, and more. You use them to control an app or Windows.

Disk Cleanup　A procedure that deletes unused content from a hard disk to optimize performance.

Drag　A procedure in which you click and hold down the left mouse button on a selected object and then move it the object another location in an app or Windows.

Driver　A program that controls settings for hardware devices such as a printer.

E

Ethernet　A group of networking technologies used to connect local area networks (LANs).

Executable file　A file that causes a computer to execute certain instructions, such as installing software on your computer. Though they have many legitimate uses, executable files can be used to spread computer viruses or download unwanted files.

F

Favorite　In Cortana, a list of favorite places used to respond to questions or searches; also, in Microsoft Edge, a list of favorite online sites.

File　A storage location for computer data related to a single document.

File Explorer　An app used to locate and manage files and folders on a Windows computer.

Flash drive　A storage device for computer data that is attached via a USB drive.

Folder　A location for a set of stored files.

G

Gesture　Movement of a finger on a touchscreen to perform an action such as scrolling or snapping windows into place.

Gigabyte　A unit of measurement for computer data representing a billion bytes.

H

Hardware Equipment related to computing such as a central processing unit (CPU), monitor, printer, and so on.

History In Microsoft Edge, a listing of recently visited sites.

HomeGroup The name for a group of computers that have been set up to access the same home network.

Home page The first webpage or pages that appear when you open a browser.

Hub The location in Microsoft Edge where you can view and edit Favorites, Reading List, History, and Downloads.

Hyperlink Code on a webpage that, when clicked or tapped, instructs the browser to go from one location on the web to another. Also used in documents to open a web location.

I

Icon A graphical representation of an item in a software program interface, such as a button.

InPrivate browsing A security feature in Microsoft Edge that you can use to browse online while blocking the downloading of cookies, temporary files, or history to your computer.

Input A method of providing data and instructions to a computer such as a mouse, keyboard, or touchscreen gesture.

Instant messaging A method of sending a real-time text message, image, or sound file to another person via a phone or messaging app on a computer.

Interface The graphical representation of apps and applications on a computer screen.

Internet A collection of computer networks that use the Internet Protocol (IP) suite to connect billions of devices around the world. The Internet supports document storage and sharing as well as access to services via the World Wide Web.

Internet service provider An entity that makes an Internet connection available to computer users.

K

Keyboard An input device that can be physical or displayed on a device's screen.

Kilobyte A unit of measurement for computer data representing one thousand bytes.

L

Laptop A form of computer that is portable and contains the central processing unit, a keyboard, mouse device, and monitor in one.

Link See *hyperlink*.

Live tile A tile located in the Windows Start menu that displays active content such as news headlines when the computer is online; a *tile* is used to open an app.

Lock A state that a computer enters that stops the user from accessing the desktop unless the user provides the appropriate password or PIN for a user account to unlock it.

Lock screen The screen that appears when a computer has been locked.

M

Magnifier   An accessibility feature that magnifies elements on the screen so that those who have low vision can more clearly see them.

Malware   A category of software that can damage data or system files of a computer or allow somebody to spy on your computing activities.

Memory   Also called primary storage, the hardware used to store data to be accessed immediately.

Menu   A feature of an operating system or software that offers commands that can be used to take actions such as saving or opening a file.

Microsoft account   An email account used to sign in to Windows to make email and other settings available to the operating system.

Microsoft Edge   A web browser built in to Windows 10.

Modem   A piece of hardware used to modulate and demodulate (hence, the term "modem") digital data transmissions to enable communications between a computer and the Internet.

N

Narrator   An accessibility feature of Windows 10 that provides audible descriptions of selections on the screen to help those who have low vision.

Navigation pane   A pane on the left side of various panels and windows in apps and Windows that offers selections for taking actions.

Network   A telecommunications setup that allows computers to communicate with one another and share data. Network data communications can occur through cables or wirelessly.

Notification   An indication of an action or reminder that appears in the Action Center of Windows. Notifications can be in regard to received emails, news stories, appointment reminders, security and maintenance alerts, and so on.

O

OneDrive   A Microsoft service for online storage and sharing of files.

Online   Having a connection to the Internet.

On-Screen Keyboard   A virtual keyboard that is displayed on your computer screen when you have activated a text box. You can use an On-Screen Keyboard by clicking keys with a mouse or by tapping on a touchscreen.

Operating system   Software that manages hardware and software functions and provides system files that enable services that support computer programs. Windows 10 is an operating system.

P

Password   A user-defined collection of characters that can include text, numbers, or punctuation to authenticate that user.

Paste   A command used to place a copy of a file or object in another location when you have cut or copied that item to the Windows clipboard.

Peripheral   A hardware device that is separate from your computer but interacts with it, such as a printer.

Picture password   The feature of Windows by which you can use a picture that you choose along with a series of gestures that you make on a touchscreen to unlock your computer.

PIN A numerical code you can use in place of a password to open a locked Windows computer. The acronym stands for Personal Identification Number.

Pin The action of attaching a shortcut to a program, website, or file to the Windows desktop or Start menu.

Playlist A feature of music players, such as the Windows Music app, that you can use to add tracks from several albums to create a customized album.

Plug-and-play Technology through which Windows recognizes peripherals that you attach to your computer and locates appropriate drivers to make them operable with little or no intervention on the part of the user.

Pointer The on-screen icon that represents the position of your mouse on a screen or in a document.

Power plan Customizable plans for how your computer handles power-draining settings such as screen brightness.

Preview pane The view in File Explorer that displays a preview of a document.

Productivity app A feature-rich application such as Microsoft Word or Excel in the Microsoft Office suite designed for users who make use of them in work-related activities.

R

Reading list A feature of the Microsoft Edge browser with which you can store online articles offline to read with or without a connection to the Internet.

Recycle Bin A folder in Windows that temporarily stores deleted files and folders before you delete them permanently.

Reset your PC A System tool that you can use to return your computer and Windows to an earlier version or reinstall Windows, keeping or removing your files in the process based on your selections.

Resolution The number of pixels displayed horizontally and vertically, which can be adjusted by a user in display settings.

Restore point A point in time when you or Windows saved your system configuration. Using System Restore, you can revert your computer to those settings, possibly overcoming problems caused by later settings.

Ribbon In some applications, a graphical toolbar offering groups of tools on tabs.

Rip The action of copying music from a storage device such as DVD to a music player on a computer.

Router A piece of networking equipment that passes data between computers on a network and the Internet.

S

Screen resolution See *resolution*.

Screen tip A label that appears identifying some on-screen elements when you hover your mouse pointer over them.

Scroll bar A bar that appears on the right side of some screens with which a computer user can scroll up or down a screen or webpage by dragging a box (called a thumb) up or down, clicking above or below the box, or clicking arrows at the top and bottom of the scroll bar.

Search box A field in which you can type a word or phrase and then perform a search for matching data.

Search engine   A program that you can use to search the Internet for information by using keywords or phrases. Bing and Google are examples of search engines.

Settings   In Windows, a group of controls with which you manage certain features such as hardware, software, and security.

Share   Pertaining to the ability to share content with others via email, social services such as Twitter, print, and other methods.

Shortcut   A graphical icon on a Windows desktop used to open an app, setting, or file/folder with a single click.

Snap   A method of quickly arranging open windows side by side on your screen.

Software   A set of instructions to your computer to direct it to perform certain actions.

Software as a Service (SaaS)   (pronounced, "sass") A method of licensing or delivering software functionality from a host location on the Internet. As Windows moves toward automatic updating of its features, it is becoming a SaaS.

Speech Recognition   An accessibility app that makes it possible for you to speak input to your computer rather than typing it.

Spyware   A type of malware that involves the downloading of code to your computer with which somebody else can observe your computing activities.

Start button   The button on the Windows taskbar that you click to open the Start menu.

Start menu   A menu in Windows 10 in which you can open installed apps on your computer, open File Explorer, Settings, or Power controls.

Subfolder   In File Explorer, a folder contained within another folder.

Swipe   To move a finger or fingers across a touchscreen computer to perform an action.

Sync   The action of coordinating files or settings among computing devices or between a computer and a service in the cloud, such as OneDrive.

System Restore   A feature of Windows that makes it possible for you to revert your computer to an earlier configuration to potentially avoid problems caused by subsequent changes in settings.

T

Tab   1) A preset horizontal spacing in a word processed document. 2) A feature of browsers that you can use to access any open webpages quickly.

Tap   On a touchscreen computer, you interact with on-screen elements by tapping the screen. This is the same as a mouse click.

Taskbar   A set of tools, minimized active programs, and menus typically located along the bottom of the Windows desktop.

Task Manager   A feature of Windows that you can use to view the status of any running processes and stop them if necessary.

Task View   A view of all active programs that makes it possible for you to move among them easily. You also can Task View to create multiple desktops.

Theme   Predesigned sets of display features such as color, background, and font, that you can apply to your Windows desktop.

This PC   A folder in File Explorer that contains files located on your computer or attached storage devices.

Tile   A graphical representation of an app located on the Start menu. See also *Live tile*.

Title bar   The strip along the top of an app containing the app name and tools such as those used to minimize, maximize, and close the app.

Toolbar   A feature of apps that contains clickable buttons for implementing commonly used functions.

U

USB   A storage device attached to a computer via a USB port, or a port on your computer to which you can connect USB devices such as a mouse or keyboard.

User account   A unique account used to sign in to Windows on a computer. Each user account can have different settings and stored documents not accessible by other users.

User interface   Also referred to as UI or graphical user interface (GUI), this refers to the visual design presented to the user of software.

V

Virus   A type of malware that, when opened, replicates itself causing damage to computer hard disks and data.

W

Web   The documents stored on the Internet in the form of webpages. Also known as the World Wide Web.

Web browser   A type of software used for navigating documents on the web.

Web Note   The ability to mark-up webpages with editing tools and share that annotated content with others.

Wi-Fi   A wireless networking technology used for sharing data among devices in the network.

Window   A rectangular element framed by a border and containing the interface of an app or application.

Windows accessories   A set of programs built in to Windows such as Paint, Snipping Tool, and WordPad to provide commonly used functionality to users.

Windows Defender   A security program that is part of Windows which provides malware protection.

Windows Firewall   When active, this program blocks access to your computer from untrusted sources over an Internet connection.

Windows Update   A feature of Windows with which you can manually or automatically download and install updates to the Windows operating system.

Index

About the author

Nancy Muir Boysen is the author of more than 100 books on technology and other nonfiction topics. Prior to her authoring career, Nancy was a senior manager at several technology publishers as well as a training manager at Symantec. She has a Certificate in Distance Learning Design from the University of Washington, and has taught Internet safety and technical writing at the university level.

2-6 99

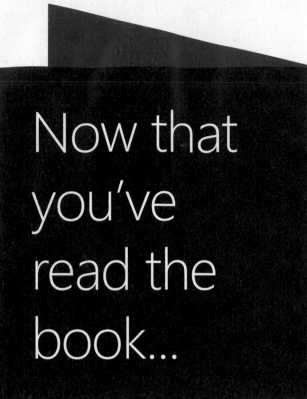

Now that you've read the book...

Tell us what you think!

Was it useful?
Did it teach you what you wanted to learn?
Was there room for improvement?

Let us know at http://aka.ms/tellpress

Your feedback goes directly to the staff at Microsoft Press, and we read every one of your responses.

Thanks in advance!